Successfully Landscaping

Your Marin Home

By: Dane E. Rose

Successfully Landscaping

Your Marin Home

By: Dane E. Rose

Cover Art by: Dane E. Rose

ISBN-13: 978-1466426481

This book is dedicated to the

people who taught me what I

know and to the clients who

give me an opportunity to

to express it.

Introduction

Creating a successful landscape has three stages that interrelate to form something bigger: A beautiful, functional garden that supports your well-being. These three stages are:

- Learning the practical aspects of landscaping.
- A design process that focuses that knowledge in alignment with your values.
- Installing your design.

This book is divided into these three sections. Section one will share 80% of the practical knowledge I use on a daily basis to create gardens that reflect my client's values. Reading it will give you confidence and possibly save you considerable amounts of time and money.

Section two will teach you how to organize this information into a cohesive and intelligent design. You will learn how to sift through the many choices available to you and identify those few that most reflect your personal values and priorities.

In part three I will walk you through the process of installing your landscape design. Should you install your landscape in stages or do it all at once? I won't tell you what to do, but will show you the pros and cons of several approaches so that you can make an informed decision.

This book includes two BONUS sections. The first is information on how to navigate your relationship with professionals. The second is a terrific mix of additional resources, including an online section with images and video links.

My goal is to save you AT LEAST $500.00 on your next landscape project of $10,000 or more. I will be brief, only going into each topic as much as is likely to be useful to 90% of you. I'll also be referring you to other free online and local resources where they are available and in areas you are likely to learn faster with a video, picture or personal demonstration.

This book is in no way a substitute for twenty years of hands-on landscape experience (many of us learn best by doing) and is certainly not comprehensive. It represents my personal landscape experience over twenty years. And since we all look for different things in a book and I want you to be happy with your purchase, that's where my money-back guarantee comes in. If you are not satisfied that this book was a good buying decision for you, simply return it to me for a full refund (see how in the chapter titled "money back guarantee").

Dane Rose

Table of Contents

Part Four: Working with Professionals

Part Five: FREE Bonus Material

Having Fun with Your Landscape

This may sound odd, coming from someone with a career in landscaping, but there are a LOT of enjoyable ways of spending time and money other than landscaping. Landscaping is far less important than your health, family and happiness. In fact the only reason to landscape IS to support your health, family and happiness!

I sometimes meet a stressed out couple trying to decide whether to spend $15,000.00 or $50,000.00 on a landscape make-over. I remind them: "Maybe what would be more fun is to go to Hawaii for two weeks to rejuvenate and have fun together with money to spare. No garden is worth straining a relationship or finances for."

And since gardens are a luxury, why not enjoy doing them? What follows are some of the common ways a landscape can stop being fun and what to do about it:

1) If you are doing too much in your life already and take on a big landscape project it's going to stress you out. **Solution:** Delay the landscape project until you have less going on, or cut back on some other focus areas in your life.
2) You have a nightmare experience with your designer and/or contractor. Perhaps you like things done on time and the project is late. Maybe things are not turning out the way you wanted them to look. **Solution:** Read the bonus chapter on successfully relating with professionals BEFORE you begin a project.
3) You feel like you are running around like a headless chicken and don't feel like you fully understand the complete costs of the entire landscape or how everything fits together. **Solution:** Create a detailed overall plan that is consistent with a clearly defined budget and go over

every aspect of the design so that you can work out any "bugs" before you begin any one stage.

4) Perhaps you and your family disagree on what to do. **Solution:** Don't push forward until you are all in agreement. Read the chapters on resolving conflict.

5) Things are costing more money than you want to or are able to spend and you or someone else in your family is stressing out about this. **Solution:** Agree on a budget within your family and stick to that. Read the chapters on how to save money, consider doing some or all of the work yourselves and be sure to negotiate carefully with any professionals you include and agree on fixed bids.

6) You don't know what you want and feel confused about how to proceed. **Solution:** First of all, there are many other things you could be doing with your life so unless you have a clear desire that results in you wanting to change your landscape then it may be simpler to do nothing. However, if you know you want something, bring in a designer with a strong communication talent to help you sort through what is and is not important to you.

7) You are reading through this book and feel overwhelmed with all there is to know and learn in order to do landscaping well. **Solution:** Recognize that this is natural. There are people who learn about landscaping their entire lives and there is still more to learn – probably a bit like some of the things you have learned to do well at work or in the home. If all the information stops being fun, you don't have to keep reading. You can always hire a good designer and relax, knowing that they know most of this stuff so you don't have to.

So have fun with your project. And remember: At the beginning of every project, before you have committed time and money, you have ALL the power to spend as much or as little as you want.

Part One:

Information You Need to Know before Designing Your Landscape

Amending Soil

Soil is extremely important. When we take good care of the soil it will care for our plants better than we possibly can. Keeping this simple, 95% of the time your soil will greatly benefit from 2-4 inches of chicken compost tilled into the surface prior to planting. Chicken compost is great for five reasons:

1) It has more nitrogen (the stuff that makes plants grow and look green) than almost any manure available.
2) It is weed-free (many manures are not).
3) It is readily available at a reasonable price in both bags and by the yard.
4) It comes mixed with composted bark that combine to make a lot of spongy organic matter, which improves water retention and helps bring oxygen into the typical heavy Marin soil.
5) It is an organic form of fertilizer that does not rely on chemicals.

You can get Chicken manure by the bag at Home Depot and other places or by the yard at American Soil in San Rafael. Because it is so high in nitrogen it will burn plants if it makes direct contact with their roots. Mix it thoroughly with 50% native soil before planting in it.

The best way to mix chicken compost with native soil is by rototilling. Before tilling, make sure that there are no irrigation lines or other utilities, such as low-voltage lighting wires, within 12" of the surface. Do this by looking carefully at the areas you plan to till and digging a few test holes with a shovel to see if you find any evidence of buried utilities.

If you are tilling steep slopes or amending soil in heavily planted areas I suggest a mini-tiller. These are much easier to operate than larger tillers. They are also considerably cheaper. For less than $400.00 you can buy a mini tiller at Home Depot with a Honda engine that works fairly well.

For large flat areas I suggest you rent a Barreto tiller. While it is large and very heavy, it can till twice as fast as any tiller I know of without throwing a belt (it utilizes hydraulic motors). You can rent a Barreto at Tam Valley Rentals in Mill Valley: (415) 383-7311 or at United Rentals in San Rafael: (415) 642-1300. Expect to spend around $100.00 for four hours and get a lot of tilling done if you are well organized.

Rototilling 2-4" of chicken compost into native soil is better than importing 8" of topsoil for several reasons:

- When amendments are tilled into native soil the roots of plants are more likely to keep growing down into the native soil when they reach the depth where the amendment stops. By contrast, when topsoil is brought in and placed on top of native soil it creates a sudden transition between two different types of soil. As a result it is more likely that plant roots will not make the transition into the native soil and will stay shallow. Shallower roots require more water and do not provide the stability of deeper roots in wind storms or heavy rains.
- When topsoil is added to native soil without rototilling, both rain-water and irrigation will penetrate the topsoil and tend to "sheet" sideways when it hits the native soil, rather than saturating the soil deeply. This in turn further discourages deep root growth. By rototilling amendment rich in organic matter into native soil water will more deeply enter the soil, encouraging roots to grow deeper.
- Spreading 2-4" of chicken compost is half the labor and cost of spreading 8" of topsoil. This can amount to a savings of thousands of dollars on the average landscape project.

If you wish to go the extra mile, you can always take soil samples of your soil and of possible amendments to determine the exact way to amend your soil. You can also opt to sprinkle various organic amendments on your soil prior to rototilling in the chicken compost.

Be aware that chicken manure smells. The more it smells, the better it is for your soil! However, out of consideration for neighbors and your own enjoyment be aware that:

- Chicken manure in bags smells less than when it is ordered by the yard.
- Don't open the bags or order the delivery until just before you are ready to spread and rototill the chicken manure in. It smells much less right after being tilled into the soil.
- Mulching your chicken compost with 2-4" of wood chips eliminates the rest of the smell. Since this is best done AFTER you plant and do any irrigation, having your plants and irrigation materials ready will allow you to eliminate the smell as quickly as possible.

On steep slopes that you rototill you may need to tamp the soil down so that it does not all fall away if it is too loose. Or you can till the first few inches and then hand mix the soil deeper in the specific planting holes. Do not amend soil except in areas you want plants to grow, as this will only encourage weeds.

Planting Plants

After you have rototilled your chicken manure into native soil, it is very easy to plant. It's best to prepare a hole 1.5-2 times bigger than your plant and then carefully put each plant in the hole. If you plant four inch and one gallon plants you will not have to "dig" much at all. Newly rototilled soil can be turned into holes just with your hand or by using a shovel to remove one large scoop of soil per plant.

If you notice that there are a lot of roots showing at the edge of the pot and that these have become bound up, use a razor-blade, shovel or your hands to loosen these roots. The goal is to have the roots loose but the soil in the pot still holding together.

Don't loosen the soil or roots if the soil is already loose and falling away from the roots. In some cases you may need to be very careful removing the plant from the pot and put the whole thing straight into the hole without touching the soil or roots, or the soil will fall completely off the roots. It is best to minimize the exposure of the roots to direct air and sunlight.

The best time to plant is in low light in the rainy season. This is more important when transplanting large plants than it is planting plants from pots. However, the time of year has such minimal impact that I would never let this stop you from planting anything any time you want to get the work done. If you are moving a ten foot tall tree, just know that it will have a 20% higher survival rate if it's moved in a November rain rather than a July hot-spell and you will have to work harder to simulate the rainy season with daily drenching's if you move it in July.

When storing plants prior to planting it is best to mass them together and minimize the direct sun exposure on the black pots. They will need to be watered daily if they are in full sun.

If you are planting in a dry month you will need to water all new plantings, including drought-tolerant plants every day for at least a month as they establish their roots. Because hand watering for a month can take more time than planting and because a lack of adequate water is the cause of 95% of all appropriately chosen plant casualties, I prefer to set up my irrigation infrastructure before planting so that all I have to do is add a dripper to each new plant the same day I put the plant in the ground. This allows the watering to be automatic from day one. However, in a dry month I will still water each plant thoroughly by hand right after planting to help compensate for the high-stress of being planted and because drip irrigation will not saturate the soil the way an overhead spray from a hose will.

You can read more about selecting your plants in the design section of the book and in the chapter on saving money.

Smart Irrigation

98% of all available plants will require at least some irrigation in the summer to look healthy. The benefits of doing this with an automatic irrigation system include:

- Freedom to go away on vacation without worrying about your plants.
- Lowering weekly maintenance.
- Making your maintenance program more precise.
- Watering things at the best time for you and the plants.
- Helping your plants planted in the dry season grow new roots with daily watering for the first month after planting.

To make an irrigation system automatic you need a timer (this tells the valve when to turn on and off), valves (these electrically turn the water on and off in each pipe when the timer specifies), pipes or hoses to transfer the water from the main line to the general area needing water, and either drip emitters or spray heads to disperse the water to individual plants.

The most important thing I'll begin with, since irrigation is such a complex subject, is where to find good advice for FREE. The Urban Farmer store in Mill Valley is more expensive than many stores in some categories to buy materials from because they build in the cost of knowledgeable and detailed advice for FREE that you rarely have to wait for.

More than any other store they have a great selection of all the MANY odds and ends required to be compatible with a variety of existing systems. You can even bring in pictures and/or a drawing of the area you want to irrigate with measurements and they will help you develop a CUSTOM plan for FREE and then help you pick out the materials you will need to put it into practice. This is a GODSEND if you are putting in a full project yourself or trying to repair or modify an existing system.

What I'll focus on here are a few tips you may or may not find at the Urban Farmer that I have found useful when installing irrigation:

- Drip irrigation is the best approach for non-lawn areas because it saves water. It also discourages weeds by watering right next to the plant you planted and nowhere else. The approach that I use is running a ½" line RIGHT UP TO EACH PLANT and then adding a drip emitter DIRECTLY into the half inch line. This takes no more time than running ¼" tubing but makes a big difference in maintenance. ¼" tubing is easily cut without noticing, can be damaged by deer, and can get plugged up with sediment.

- Always place your drippers UP HILL of your plants so that the water runs downhill towards the plant.

- Bury your irrigation valves in a VALVE BOX so you don't have to look at them and to prolong their life by avoiding direct sunlight. (As these notes are intended in addition to help from the Urban Farmer or an irrigation specialist don't worry if you don't understand the terms at this point. You can read these notes again later when you know more.)

- Consider using a SMART TIMER for your irrigation. In the last few years special timers have become available that gather weather information DAILY from your site and then use that information to water just enough for your specific plants. This is estimated to save as much as 30% off your water bill and can also eliminate the need to periodically adjust or turn off your irrigation timer. It is all done automatically and the cost of these is getting lower and lower. The Marin Municipal Water District is now requiring new landscapes to use smart timers, although this is not being rigorously enforced at this time.

- Put together a mini irrigation installation and/or repair box with 2-5 of everything you might need. Drip heads pop off sometimes. Solenoid valves can go bad periodically. Drip lines are accidentally cut and need to be reconnected. Having all the parts you need in a handy box saves water, keeps plants alive and most importantly of all it means your repairs will get done because you have the part on hand. Expect to spend about $100.00 for this and make it back by not having to call out a professional and in saved water.

That's it. These few tips alone can save you hundreds to thousands of dollars over time. I asked the Urban Farmer if they would include a coupon in the coupon section so remember to use that if you decide to go there.

And in case you're wondering, they have not paid me any money for my recommendation and I only shop there when it's conveniently near a job. However, it's the only place I would shop if I was a home-owner and did not know what I was doing.

Mulching

Mulching is one of those wonderful things that does multiple things for you simultaneously. It's as if you hired a house-cleaner who changed the oil in your car, painted the house and washed the windows for FREE!

Some of the things mulch does for you include:

- Protects your soil from eroding away in heavy rains.
- Hides drip irrigation and low-voltage lighting lines and protects them from sunlight.
- Insulates the soil from extreme temperatures, protecting marginal plants from frost damage and preventing soil-cracking in full sun.
- Helps the soil retain 25% more water.
- Discourages weed seeds from germinating by blocking light. If you spread bark RIGHT AFTER rototilling (see previous chapter) you may eliminate 50% of your weeds before they even germinate!
- Adds color contrast to green leaves.
- Makes things look neater by adding a uniform texture.
- Provides food for worms and micro-organisms as it breaks down.
- Minimizes soil-compaction as a result of foot-traffic and, heavy rains and watering.

There are many types of mulches. As long as it is organic, free of weed-seed and not rich in nitrogen it will do the things stated above. I typically use a shredded redwood (sometimes called "gorilla hair") when on a steep slope (it will not wash away as easily as other mulches). On flat areas I use the smallest bark (sometimes called "micro-bark" or "ground-cover bark") available because it lets in less air and light than a chunk bark. Air and light encourage weeds.

Most Marin gardens are small so I also like the fact that by using a smaller bark it creates a miniature scale which makes other things look bigger around it.

For all these reasons one of the most important things you can do as preventative maintenance is to mulch. After you have established a 2-3" layer of mulch, adding one inch of mulch every year will keep things looking and smelling fresh. As mulch bio-degrades at a rate of approximately 1" per year this will maintain your mulch cover indefinitely.

American Soils in San Rafael is one place to get a wide variety of mulches, including micro-bark. Home depot and other stores have bark by the bag. OSH in San Rafael has quick help loading bags of bark in their drive-through. Micro-bark is also sometimes called "ground-cover bark."

Landscape Lighting

Many of us spend more time at home after dark than during daylight hours. After spending tens of thousands of dollars to create a beautiful landscape, not being able to see it at night is a terrible waste. Spending less than 10% more on a landscape can double the enjoyment we receive from our landscape when applied to landscape lighting.

Other benefits of landscape lighting include:

- Safety and comfort on pathways and stairs.
- Discouraging unwanted animal visitors.
- Adding to home-security at night.

There is one instance where landscape lighting does not make sense: Because almost all real-estate transactions occur during daylight hours it is not a good investment to install landscape lighting SOLELY for the purpose of selling your home.

This chapter deals with information that is NOT on the packages and instructions that commonly come with low-voltage fixtures and lighting kits. If you are totally new to electrical wiring I suggest you begin by either doing a YouTube search on "low voltage lighting" and "low voltage electrical wiring" or visit the Urban Farmer in Mill Valley, where they will answer any questions you may have. The Urban Farmer provides unusually helpful information as well as a unique service of loaning out a lighting kit at no charge to allow you to test them in your landscape before making any commitment to purchase. This provides confidence that the fixtures you buy will create the lighting result you want. The Urban Farmer has higher prices and better quality than Home Depot and many other local suppliers. Home Depot has the lowest landscape lighting costs and hopeless customer service, which is a problem if you don't know what you are doing.

There are three types of lighting choices available:

- High-voltage lights (110 volts, just like your house).
- Low voltage lights.
- Solar lights.

Typically it makes sense to use high-voltage lights when the fixtures are attached directly to your house and/or when you want to use high-powered flood lights that require more than around fifty watts of light. High voltage lights are typically three to five times more expensive to install and are simultaneously more dangerous if a wire gets cut or a connection gets wet. Because of that, you want to have a good reason to do it. In the case of fixtures attached directly to a house, they may be easier to control from an indoor switch or a motion sensor (there are still relatively few motion sensor options for low-voltage lights). In the second case, if you want to easily generate 100 or more watts from one fixture, you can easily install high voltage fixtures with 1500 or more watts to light up the side of a house, a large tree or a sports area. A licensed electrician or a home-owner is legally required to install high-voltage lighting. An electrician may be required if it the project is beyond what you feel comfortable with.

High voltage light-bulbs come in the form of incandescent, compact florescent, halogen and LED.

Switching high voltage lights can be done in several ways:

- By plugging a radio switched outlet into an existing electrical outlet and then plugging your lights into that. You can then turn lights on and off using the radio control switch (no electrician required). Some radio control switches are hand held and fit easily on a key-chain. Others are designed to look like a normal interior light switch. These can typically be mounted with a sticker or screws on any portion of your wall. In this scenario you will need to periodically change the battery that powers your radio control switch.

- Plugging lights into an outlet that is linked to an indoor hard-wired switch allows you to turn your high voltage lights on and off by turning that switch manually.
- You can have a new wired switch and an outlet added by an electrician and plug your lights into this if you do not have one already.
- You can also use a combination of electrical timer and/or light sensor to automatically turn your lights on and off. For example the lights could go on as soon as it got dark (this varies throughout the year and it is annoying to keep adjusting the timer) and then turn off at midnight.

Costs: You can expect to spend between $25-$300.00 per high-voltage fixture, depending on what you buy. If you do not involve an electrician the cost of the switching materials for all of the above options is normally less than $100.00 per light set-up. If you involve an electrician you might spend, on average, anywhere from $300-$1,800.00. The variables include whether or not an extra circuit-breaker is required, how far the wire needs to run, the location of the switch and what types of walls or soil the wires need to run through.

Low voltage lights are great for several reasons:

- Inexpensive to buy and repair.
- A wide range of fixtures available.
- Low risk of electrical shock installing or maintaining them.
- Easy to install yourself if you want to save money.
- In many cases the wires can run on the surface of the ground, saving labor trenching.
- Kits are readily available with complete installation instructions that are geared for the home-owner.

Low voltage light bulbs come in the form of halogen, incandescent and LED. Halogen bulbs are typically a brighter and warmer light with bulbs costing around $6.00 per bulb. In the last year LED bulbs online have come down to match this price and are now the only sensible way to go. You can find them listed on a site sponsored by Mystical Landscapes at www.MarinGardener.org. LED bulbs take three to four times less power, are not as hot and last longer. This in turn allows you to put more fixtures on a smaller wire and transformer, which all adds up to an amazing improvement in lighting options that saves you money while benefiting the environment. Switching:

- Low voltage lighting kits typically come with a transformer that has a built-in timer. This allows you to automatically set up what time the lights turn on and off EVERY day (most timers don't allow different times on different days). As this method is built in at no extra charge it is the easiest way to switch your low voltage lights.
- You can add a light sensor to the above set up and set the timer to turn on at 4:30pm and off at whatever time you want it to go off. With the light-sensor in place the lights will not turn on at 4:30pm but when it gets dark, regardless of what time it is. When combined with the timer they will not stay on until dawn, but turn off whenever the timer shuts them off.
- You can also use any of the switched or radio-controlled switch options mentioned in the section on high-voltage light switching.

The light or the fixture?

There is an important value choice for you to make when it comes to low-voltage lighting. On the low end, you can buy inconspicuous basic black fixtures for around $18.00 each. Here the focus is on the light itself, with the fixture being largely invisible and fairly cheap. On the other hand you can have custom or very fancy fixtures in the $50-$400.00 range per fixture. These are usually better made AND are often not only providers of light, but serve as decorative accents.

Expensive fixtures often come with a good warranty plan. However, as you will need to pay shipping costs, take it back to the store or in many cases mail it to the manufacturer and wait weeks, it is sometimes easier just to buy a new low-cost fixture than it is to repair an expensive old one.

There is also the fact that ALL low cost and expensive fixtures that have glass between the light bulb and landscape need to be cleaned with vinegar and a paper towel every year or so. Water builds up on the glass and then evaporates with the light, leaving a milky mineral deposit that starts to impede the passage of light.

Personally, I find it more hassle than it's worth to track warranty information and receipts for a simple fixture. I'd rather just put in a new fixture than box up the old one, ship it off and wait three weeks. Given that the more expensive fixtures typically cost three times or more what a basic black metal fixture costs, I usually just buy a few extra basic fixtures any time I put in a system and keep a few extras as spares to leave with the client. It takes only a few minutes to swap out a fixture, which is less time than it takes to go to the post office to send it back to warranty. Normally the only time I use high-end fixtures is if a client is excited by a particular fixture and/or if the fixtures are going to be built into a deck, wall or steps in ways that make them harder to swap out and/or more visible.

Costs: You can buy basic low-voltage lighting kits with 4-15 fixtures included ranging from $100-$300.00 online, at Home Depot or other landscape supply centers. You can assemble your own kit and expect to pay 30% more for similar fixtures.

Solar powered lights are the cheapest to buy and install by far, but have several drawbacks:

- The range of available fixtures is minimal.
- The light produced is typically two to ten times less than a corresponding low-voltage fixture.
- The light is almost always a cold silver/white.
- They only work well when placed in full sun the previous day.
- The places that need the most light are typically in shady areas which do not get enough sun to power them.
- They will not usually last more than a few hours after dark – not a good choice for an all-night light.
- You cannot turn them on and off by a central switch.

The drawbacks of solar lights are such that I have never chosen to use them so far. I might use them in locations where there was no easy power-source and to give a general sense of direction on paths where people had flashlights if they needed more light.

Deer Management

There are three main ways that deer can cause damage or be a nuisance in a garden:

- Eating your plants.
- Pooping on the lawn and other areas.
- Damaging trees and shrubs as bucks attempt to rub the velvet off of newly emerging horns.

The most straightforward approach to all potential deer problems is to fence them out of all or a portion of your garden. A seven foot high transparent fence, which can be constructed of wire and netting attached to various frameworks, or an opaque six foot high fence will generally do the job. Variations on this can include a four foot transparent fence placed immediately on top of a three foot wall, creating a total jump height of seven feet. Depending on your budget it is possible to create any of a number of fence types, including wrought iron. Avoid leaving gaps wider than six inches.

The second strategy is more involved and experimental. Bucks tend to want to scrape the velvet from their horns in winter/spring. Mini-fences five feet tall or sticking six foot long bamboo stakes in the ground around the tree every four inches during this period usually works. Creating a garden that features stone, art and sculpture and deer resistant plants takes' care of the biggest problem, which is plants being eaten.

It's important to be aware that deer will eat almost any plant if there is no alternative – even plants on most deer proof lists. To know what the deer are eating in your neighborhood pay attention to your neighbors and what is working for them. What is eaten a mile away may not be eaten in your garden and vice versa. The list of plants I have never seen a deer eat grows ever smaller!

It is often a combination of factors that ensure that a deer does not eat a specific plant, any one of which may not be enough alone. Having a dog helps, along with being closer to town in higher-traffic areas. A pet lion would almost certainly do the trick, although lions have been known to produce serious side effects on human health (being eaten not being the least among these).

Plants closer to a house will tend to be bothered less than plants further away and deer are somewhat discouraged by having to walk up steps or over decks that make a lot of noise, but this is a minor deterrent that can in no way be counted on. Then there are the various commercial deer deterrents, such as liquid fence, soaps and socks filled with blood-meal. While all of these things discourage deer, it all depends on how hungry they are and whether or not there is easier food nearby. Your job is to make the deer dining facilities of your garden less attractive than the establishments offered by your neighbors, as deer rarely pay their bills and are lousy tippers.

Reflectors and moving shiny objects also play a role in deterring deer from entering areas by jumping. I have seen instances where deer were jumping over a four foot gate inside an arch, but stopped when a decorative piece of shiny cloth was hung from the arch so that a deer would have to touch it as they jumped over the gate. Deer prefer not to jump towards shiny moving objects.

A short list of deer resistant plants with year-round interest:
(Add to this list by talking with knowledgeable nursery staff.)

- Mexican and other sages
- Acorus Gramineus
- Rosemary
- Creeping lantana
- Yuka
- Coleonema

- Lavender
- Daphne
- Miscanthus and many other ornamental grasses
- Sedum (and all other succulents/cactus)
- Japanese boxwood
- Phormiums
- Loropetalum "Plum Delight"
- Polystickum ferns
- Santolina
- Tulbaghia violacea "variegate"
- Rhododendrons
- Sasanqua Camellias
- Oak leaf Hydrangeas

Minimizing Mole Damage

Moles present the biggest problem in lawn areas, where they will often burrow sixty feet of tunnels a day, causing portions of the lawn to collapse into ruts with time and an endless amount of ongoing holes and mounds of soil. These potentially interfere with irrigation spray patterns.

The very best way to preclude mole damage to a lawn or planting bed is to lay down galvanized wire-mesh with a ½" grid (or less). Stapling this down with drip irrigation staples (make sure to overlap the fencing at least 6" where pieces intersect) and then adding ½" of soil on top of this before laying sod or seeding does the job. In bed areas you will need to cut holes in it to plant plants (be aware they may come up right in the hole you cut for each plant).

I'm not as bothered with moles making mounds of soil in beds because they blend in with the bark, so I typically only put down the fencing below a lawn. This can be added retro-actively by de-sodding a lawn and then re-sodding on top of the mesh but is obviously much cheaper done before the original sod is placed.

Chemicals and smoke bombs and filling tunnels with water is close to useless, in my experience. Given that a mole can tunnel sixty feet a day they can probably out-tunnel these deterrents and I've never noticed any effect.

The underground noise makers available work intermittently. You will need three times as many mole-chasers (one of the products) as the manufacturer claims are required for a twenty five hundred square foot area. Plan on getting one per seven hundred square feet. The rattlers work better than the beepers in my experience. You will need to use them forever and change the batteries every 3-6 months or the moles will likely return. Allow thirty days for them to take effect.

Screening and Fencing

Fencing is used to contain or keep out animals and/or people, while screening is used for privacy or to block an ugly view. These two are linked together because fencing is one form of screening and some screens can make effective fences.

Fencing for deer: See requirements in previous chapter.

Fencing for dogs: You first need to know how high your dog(s) can jump. The next step is to determine how large an area is needed and where you want to contain the dog(s). If your dog is a digger, the fencing may need to be dug into the ground 6"-12". If not, it can start a few inches off the ground. The gaps in the fence will need to be just smaller than the smallest dog you own can squeeze through.

Dog fences do not need to be at the edge of a garden. Depending on the purpose and the dog you can simply fence off certain planting areas rather than fence the dog in or you can create a meandering fence that follows a pathway etc.

Fencing for children: Fences only work effectively for children under the age of about six. After that any determined child can find a way over a garden fence so the purpose of fencing is to slow movement down and discourage spontaneous activity, such as running out to the street after a ball.

Types of fences: If your fence is going to be visually prominent I suggest you put a bit of thought into the design. It typically only takes 30% more money to make a mediocre wood fence look great. That money could be spent doing interesting painting, trim detail or simply creating an interesting pattern in the board layout. For ideas do a Google image search for fences. Below are a few basic types.

Wood Fences: A basic framework of pressure treated posts and horizontal 2"x4"s can be used to support a variety of boards. You typically want your support posts to be between 4'-8' apart, depending on the height of the fence, how deep the posts are buried and how much concrete you use in the holes. A fence forms a large wind-sail, which means that it has to be well-anchored in the ground – 2' deep or more for solid six foot fences.

- Consider "grape stakes" as one possible inexpensive rustic fence design.
- If using a solid board design, inserting 1" lathes in a pattern can make a typically solid fence significantly more distinctive.

Metal Fences: The price of prefabricated white or black metal fences has become so low at places such as Home Depot that it is well worth considering.

Wire fences: The cheapest and easiest fence to install uses metal "T" posts (farmers use these and they are readily available at most hardware stores) and a post-pounder. For a six foot fence use 8' posts and then attach typical farm fencing material to these posts. The fact that it is so inexpensive can save money that can be used to plant shrubbery in front of the fence and/or vines on the fence.

Ideas for screens: Screening is best incorporated into an overall design, rather than treated separately. The most attractive and interesting screens are sometimes not all made of one thing. For example, screening to block a neighbor's house might be simultaneously achieved by addressing your goals for a garden shed and shade. If it makes sense, locate your shed in a position that blocks part of the view and a shade tree next to the shed to continue the screening. This could be connected to a small section of fence, several tall shrubs or an art wall to fill in any visual gaps.

Terracing With Walls

The typical do-it-yourself (and many professionally built) retaining walls are often made of basic wood. While straight-forward, this has a number of down-sides, in my opinion:

- Basic wood walls rarely looks as nice as stone.
- Wood does not last as long as stone.
- Basic wood does not add as much property value as stone.
- Wood is straight, creating angles rather than curves.
- Wood destroys forests.
- Wood is not any cheaper than stone and so does not justify these downsides with cost.

Most of the walls I build are dry-stack stone walls using Sonoma Fieldstone. This particular stone is locally available, which makes it very inexpensive and ecologically sound. While it is no nicer than many stones (and not as nice as some) it is 2-5 times less expensive than most available stone, which makes it almost as inexpensive to build with as wood.

A dry-stack stone wall maintains the existing drainage pattern on the site without requiring any additional drainage. This is a huge benefit over wood and concrete retaining walls that often do require drainage. These artificial drainage systems concentrate the water on site to one place, which is also not ideal because it leads to the question of where to direct that concentrated water. Most of the answers cost money and some make for an unhappy downhill neighbor.

For decorative purposes you can build dry-stack, cement or other walls away from unstable slopes up to 3'11" tall without needing a permit or structural engineer. Since it is not something easily written about, it's best to go to you-tube and search under "dry stack stone wall building." Currently there is even a video of someone building with Sonoma Fieldstone!

Wall stone is best ordered by the pallet. At present time American Soils in San Rafael offers the best price/selection of Sonoma fieldstone so I typically buy from them. Pallet deliveries arrive on a truck with a fork-lift on the back. I buy from Shamrock when there is challenging site access and/or a steep hill because their forklift at the present time is superior to all other forklifts I am aware of and well worth the extra money to have the pallets dropped exactly where I want them. Sometimes most of my profit building a wall comes from winning an argument with a forklift operator who initially does not want to work their machine a bit harder just to save me several days' labor hauling large rocks an extra one hundred or more feet up a steep hill! Unless you know a lot about forklifts and what they are capable of it's probably best to go along with the operator, but you'll have more options with Shamrock.

Grading the Site

The best designs work with the existing site to create the look and functions you need with a minimum of unnecessary change. Nevertheless, you will sometimes need to bring in or export large quantities of soil or dramatically reconfigure the soil that is there.

This is definitely an area to consider as a whole. You don't want to design the front yard and export thirty yards of soil only to import forty yards of soil when you get around to designing the back yard five years later. Because bringing in and removing soil can be expensive and a hassle, I have trained my mind to consider removal and placement options simultaneously. When I'm designing a large pond, I'm thinking about what area in the garden would most benefit from a higher mound or extending the level area on a slope.

On large grading projects it's also valuable to understand heavy equipment and costs. People tend to design within their comfort zones and this can be a mistake. For example, it can be cheaper in some instances to both lower a large area and create a six foot privacy mound with the soil than it is to build a fence there, but if you are not experienced with heavy equipment and do know a bit about fencing your mind will tend to overlook options like this, or proceed to spend weeks doing something by hand that can be done in a day with a large machine. I realize that saying this is not very encouraging, since you have probably not operated a bulldozer, backhoe or excavator, but it's one of the reasons I encourage you to have an experienced designer and/or installer review your plans even if you are going to do the work yourself. It would be a shame to spend months doing something by hand that could have been done for less in a few days with the right equipment.

Grading ties into a number of areas of landscaping, including terracing with retaining walls (it's usually best to grade first or parallel with any walls being built), drainage, possible permits, large water-features, some aspects of demolition and soil amendment. In the case of soil amendment, it's helpful to put the topsoil off to the side and spread it back on top of the finished grade, as some sub-soils in Marin are dead, rocky and very difficult for plants to grow in.

Keep in mind that grading can also be interchangeable with retaining walls and can be cheaper. If you are putting in a four foot path perpendicular to a slope it would be normal to think in terms of cutting into the slope to form the path and building a small retaining wall on the uphill side of the path. When machinery is present it may be much faster and cheaper to slightly steepen the upper and lower slope without using any stone. If stone is used, one row of rocks to help define the path may replace a three foot wall that would have been necessary if the areas ten feet to the up and down hill sides of the path had not been graded.

Grading is a very important design element because it determines the views, shapes, scale and sense of space within the landscape more than many other things.

Water Features

Water features will often cost more per square foot to build and maintain than any other area of your landscape. What this means is that they need to bring you more value per square foot than any other aspect of your landscape to justify that cost. For many people they do. I have clients who feel so comforted by the sound of their water-features outside their bedroom windows that they literally CANNOT sleep when it stops working.

Water-features offer a number of values:

- Noise buffering to block street and neighbor noise, as well as provide privacy for conversation.
- Movement in a largely still landscape.
- Relaxation and stress-relief.
- Night beauty when lit at night.
- Fun for birds/wildlife.

The very cheapest way to introduce water into your landscape is with the use of a prefabricated above-ground kit. You can find these at a variety of garden centers, from Target to Sloats and OSH. They typically cost between $200-$2,000.00 depending on the size and where you buy them from. The biggest challenge with this type of water-feature is usually keeping them filled with water so the pump does not burn up. If you are experiencing algae growth you can treat the water similarly to a swimming pool, using pool chemicals at the same ratio per gallon of water as you would for a swimming pool – or a bit less.

Custom water features are both a lot more exciting and a different ball game altogether. Don't do a custom water-feature unless you are willing to do it well or it will become an expensive headache. If installing a custom water-feature yourself expect to spend between $1,200.00 and $2,500.00 in materials. You will also need to bring an electrical outlet within ten feet of your pond. Once installed, expect to spend $15-60.00 per month in electrical costs for lights and pump operation, depending on the size of your pump and how efficient it is.

YouTube is a good place to start learning about pond construction. You can watch a variety of pond-building techniques that will give you more of a feeling for the process than fifty pages of text.

Below are important elements to include in your custom water-feature. They will increase your visual enjoyment, add longevity and lower maintenance:

- Using 45 mm EPDM liner will make your installation process easier than many other liner types. It may need protection both below and above in the form of thick drainage fabric or used carpet. This is particularly important if you have deer, as a hoof inside a pond can puncture the liner if it is not protected.
- Build your pond at least 2' deep in the middle. This will allow it to stay cooler in the summer, minimizing algae growth. In the event you have fish, this also gives them a place to hide below the reach of birds and raccoons.
- Lights are always a great idea. Low-voltage lights can be placed underwater shining up at any waterfalls or fountains. Or they can be placed at the edge of the pool shining towards any features you want to highlight.
- Use a skimmer box. This does a number of things:
  o It catches many leaves, slowing down build-up on the bottom of the pond.
  o It houses the pump, prolonging its life and making pump-maintenance easier.
  o It can house an auto-inflow valve (which I recommend) and keep this out of view.
  o It houses a small filter, which helps maintain the clarity of your water.

- Install an auto-inflow valve. This functions similarly to a toilet float. When evaporation, splashing and animals drinking from the pond lowers the water level, it automatically refills it to the desired level. This protects your pump from burning out and saves you the chore of adding water manually.
- Use an energy-efficient pump. An energy efficient pump may cut your power down by half. Given that this may save you hundreds of dollars in electrical bills, it is well-worth the extra $30-$130.00 for a better pump.
- Make sure that your water moves briskly. Stagnant water breeds mosquitos. A good pump, fountain and/or waterfall will accomplish this. Don't turn off your pump for more than twelve hours at a time.

Where to place your pond? Since it is an expensive part of your landscape the best place is somewhere it will bring the most value. An entranceway or an area in the back-garden where it can be heard and seen through many windows are two ideal locations. Other considerations include:

- Placing it between you and noise you want to mask.
- Placing it near an existing power-source (this may save you $500-$2,000.00 in electrical costs).
- Placing it in the shade (this helps minimize algae growth).

Most of the pools I put in function fine with about 15 minutes a week in maintenance. This is spent cleaning the filter, emptying the skimmer net and changing the occasional light-bulb. A well-designed infrastructure does the rest. In some cases a client forgets about the pond for months without any problems but a weekly check-up is best.

If algae is a problem it can be treated in three ways:

- Building up an ecology of plants and/or fish – particularly plants such as water-lilies that lower the light-level in the water (sunlight feeds algae).
- Increasing the flow of the water (this is particularly important if you have fish).
- Treating the pond (assuming there are no fish) with chlorine tablets, which can be found at a pool-supply store. These slow release tablets need to be added about every month. In high concentrations they make the water unhealthy to drink for dogs, cats and birds, so it's best not to have to add chemicals at all by beginning with a good design.

Useful facts:

- The bigger a water-feature/pond is the lower the cost per square foot.
- Large ponds typically use less water than an irrigated lawn of the same size.

Solving Drainage Issues

Drainage is a creative arena. There is only one rule and a thousand ways to apply it. The rule: Since water always goes downhill your job is to make it easier for water to go down the hill you want it to than any other hill available to it.

Ways of doing this include:

- Putting a mound in its natural path, such that it is easier for the surface water to flow somewhere else.
- Digging a trench or ditch in its natural path and running that downhill to a desired location.
- Digging a trench and filling that trench with gravel and perforated pipe and running that to a desired location.
- Directing water to an open or enclosed pit and from there pumping it with a sump pump.
- Grading the soil so that it slopes away from things you wish to keep dry.
- Raising something so that it is above the natural water-table.
- Adding a slope to an area that is too wet so that water can easily run off.
- Minimizing the use of artificial irrigation to keep an area dry.
- Planting evergreen trees. Trees can absorb up to 2,000 gallons of water a day from the soil and disperse them into the atmosphere.
- When filling in a hole or raising the soil level put a layer of sand, gravel or waste bricks/concrete and cover this with drainage fabric before adding the soil. This will increase drainage significantly but may not be necessary.
- In lawns you can add catch basins with surface grates to pipe surface water away.

I encourage you to be creative. As long as you make it slightly easier for water to flow the way you want it to, it will. Water is lazy and will always take the path of least resistance. For more visual ideas search you-tube under such topics as:

- Building a French Drain
- Installing Drainage
- Installing catch basins.

One thing to consider as part of an overall landscape plan is gutter water. If your home currently deposits the water from your roof on the ground near the house, consider the following:

- Does it have an easy place to flow away from the house?
- Is it doing any erosion damage?
- Is it swamping an area of lawn or plants?

It is ideal to collect all gutter run-off in in 4" drainage pipes well away from any area it might cause a problem – preferably to the street. If it cannot be run to the street there are other options, such as running it to a gravel-filled trench where it can be dispersed. PVC straight pipe (usually white) is far preferable to the corrugated black pipe that is often used. The latter gets clogged easily, is not as strong and can be damaged when clearing out a block.

Plumbing for drainage using PVC is similar to plumbing irrigation pipes, with the main difference being that everything is much bigger, from the glue cans to the pipe. By the time you have mastered basic irrigation you will probably feel fairly comfortable with drainage. Jackson's Hardware in San Rafael and Goodman's Ace Hardware in Mill Valley have an unusually good selection of drainage fittings, as well as the normal pipes that are common at most hardware stores and building supply stores.

Landscaping Sustainably

Living sustainably or being "Green" has become popular and many companies have jumped on the band-wagon. Often it can appear that to "be green" you need to buy new things or redo your garden. This is rarely the case, and without taking a position on whether or not a garden should be sustainable I'll outline three levels of sustainability.

But first, what is a totally sustainable landscape? Very simply it is a landscape that does not require ANY artificial energy source from outside. Nature is the only truly sustainable landscape.

Level One: Just to put things in perspective, the VERY best thing for the environment in most cases is to do absolutely nothing. Turn off all irrigation, disconnect any power, stop mowing, weeding and anything else. In a matter of months or years your garden will become overgrown in a mix of plants that require no maintenance in order to survive and provide habitat for native animals.

Level Two: The next level of sustainability in most cases is to minimally maintain what already exists. To illustrate this let's examine the energy consumed in the process of taking a few hundred square feet of concrete or asphalt and turning it into a bed with drought-tolerant ground-cover. In Marin this process might go something like this:

- One or more designers meet with the client on site as the client decides who to work with. Assuming two meetings with two different designers let's allow two hours for round trip travel. Five gallons of gas are now in the air.

- The designer and client meet again to discuss the design (another trip with 1-3 cars involved depending on whether the client is home and whether it is a couple and they drive separate cars or not). Let's assume two gallons of gas are now in the air.

- The designer stops off at a supplier to buy marking paint, drafting pencils etc. to be prepared. These have been manufactured and shipped to the store from out of state. Let's assume twenty gallons of water are used in manufacturing, two gallons of fuel, and another gallon in transportation.

- After the design is agree on another meeting may take place to sign a contract, printed on paper from trees. Let's assume another three gallons of gas.

- The concrete is removed with a jack-hammer and debris box. The jack hammer consumes several gallons worth of fuel in the process, a special trip was made to the site, the jack-hammer consumed one thousand gallons of water being manufactured, and the steel tip in the jack-hammer has been shipped from out of state and typically wears out on a concrete job. Replacing the steel tip may consume twenty gallons of water and ten gallons of gas.

- A large truck comes and hauls the concrete to a waste facility, consuming five gallons of gas. The concrete is crushed into a crusher by a machine that used several hundred thousand gallons of water to be manufactured, plus shipping, plus lots of energy/gas.

- While the concrete crushing machine is running water is sprayed constantly into the air at the San Rafael transfer station to control the dust, using approximately 50 gallons of water during the time this concrete is crushed.

- The driver of the machine and the truck drove in to work, consuming several gallons of gas that goes into the air.

- Another truck comes in to get the crushed concrete and takes it somewhere else.

- The ground-cover gets trucked in to a nursery and from there to the site. It has been grown in plastic pots, consuming oil. It has typically been treated with petroleum based fertilizer and planted in soil that has been trucked into the nursery, consuming further energy.

- Bark and compost gets trucked in to the job-site to mulch the plants. This bark subsidizes paper and lumber costs as a waste product and does not end up on the ground the trees were removed from, which contributes to soil depletion.

- An irrigation system may or may not be involved but typically is to get even drought-tolerant plants established. It is made from plastic, derived from oil.

And all of this and a lot more is done so that an area of concrete can now have plants in it. And to maintain these plants a maintenance company will often drive over several times a month and then top off the bark from time to time. Then these plants may last 3-10 years before typically being replaced with new ground-cover or some new idea, which starts the process all over again.

There is a very good argument that a) Investing in better design up front and not having the concrete there in the first place to remove and b) that leaving many things as they are is better for the environment than major changes to make the landscape more environmentally friendly. And certainly when taking into account the high cost of landscaping in Marin, it would benefit the environment a hundred times more to contribute $1,000.00 to a charity that buys and conserves rainforests than to spend $10,000.00 in an environmental landscape makeover.

The bottom line: Most changes we do only make sense if they bring the property owner more personal pleasure than the cost and are done for that reason.

Level Three: The third level of sustainability is what most of us talk about and mean when we say we are doing things sustainably. When we create the garden we want but do so in ways that are sensitive to our impact on the environment we are operating at this level. Using the example in level two of removing the concrete, it is much more sustainable to put in drought tolerant ground-cover than it is to replace it with a big concrete waterfall that runs with lights and pump twenty four hours a day.

Below are things that you can incorporate into your landscape design that move in the direction of sustainability:

Drought Tolerant Plants: Planting drought tolerant plants in the late fall and watering them as necessary through the first summer (or with some plants once or twice during peak-summer time) saves water and eliminates the need for a plastic and metal intensive irrigation system.

Synthetic Turf: The benefit of synthetic turf, relative to the environment, is that it eliminates the need for irrigation and installing an irrigation system, as well as mowing. The downside to the environment is:

- Does not absorb storm run-off as well as sod and requires plastic drainage infrastructure as a result.

- Manufacturing the plastic for the synthetic turf pollutes the air and is energy intensive.

- It is often shipped from further away than natural sod, increasing shipping energy.

- When synthetic sod gets tired, as any plastic eventually does outdoors, it must be disposed of in a land-fill, whereas sod can be composted, or covered over with new sod/plants.

- It eliminates biological habitat.

- It competes with turf and seed farms which have a positive impact on air quality, relative to home-development or factories.

Smart Irrigation: Read about this in the irrigation chapter. Smart irrigation timers can eliminate around 30% of water over other timers.

Animal Habitat: Assuming that bio-diversity is generally good for the environment, a landscape can create habitat and food for a variety of creatures:

- Birds through fruit, nuts, seeds and nectar.

- Bees and insects through flowers, fruits, seeds and nectar.

- Raccoons through fruit and shrubbery.

- Deer with lawn, fruit and plants deer like to graze on.

- Non-treated water-features as drinking sources for all animals.

- Mosquitos by allowing stagnant pools of water to sit. (OK, OK, I'm having a bit of fun with you.).

Avoiding Chemicals: Avoiding pesticides and other toxic chemicals is one of the best ways to protect birds, insects, water sources and the animals that drink these. This is also safer for human health.

Maximizing Green Areas: As far as soil, air-quality and animal habitat is concerned, the more plants the better. It is often ideal for every bit of rain and sun to touch a leaf before the soil.

Native Plants: Some native plants are both drought tolerant and provide habitat or food for local animals. There are plenty of non-native plants that do this as well. Some people believe it is better for the environment to use only natives.

Erosion Control: By densely planting and mulching steep slopes it helps to protect the soil and improve air and local water quality. The more plants absorb or slow down run-off the less city infrastructure is required to expensively treat or transfer water to the bay.

Soil Health: When the soil is healthy, so are the plants and the animals and people who eat the plants. Keeping a soil healthy includes avoiding chemicals, adding organic matter and mulching to protect soil from erosion and direct sunlight.

LED Light Bulbs: LED bulbs consume two to five times less power, last two to ten times longer and require smaller wires and a smaller transformer to run. From select suppliers they have now dropped to the same price in some cases as Halogens, making them a no-brainer for your wallet and the environment.

Maximizing Real Estate Value

How much should I spend? While every home-buyer is a unique individual, as a statistic 80% of the market will pay between 5%-15% more for a home that is tastefully and functionally landscaped. You will also get the most value for your home when the home, location and neighborhood are in balance. If your landscape is already nicer than your home you will get a greater return by renovating the home than you will spending more on your landscape, and vice versa. If your home and/or landscape is nicer than your neighborhood already investing more in your home or landscape may not be a good idea from an investment standpoint.

What kinds of returns can I expect from landscape investments? This depends largely on three things:

- The quality of your design.

- Whether or not the landscape is currently the most underdeveloped of your home, neighborhood and landscape.

- How easy it is for a buyer to imagine landscaping an area or solving a landscape challenge.

Design is the most important aspect of your landscape. You can spend the exact same amount of money implementing a poor design as you do implementing an exceptional design. Poor designs often cost even more by overlooking site-opportunities and imposing an expensive plan that does not fit the site. When a home-buyer pays more for a nice landscape they don't do it based on what that landscape cost you to build it. They do it based on the value it brings to them, relative to what else is on the market.

If you have a beautiful home in a beautiful neighborhood and a sloppy or non-existent landscape, installing a tasteful design could instantly bring twice as much value to your home as the cost of the landscape, while simultaneously making your home more attractive to buy. Realtors and appraisers agree that on similar homes with similar prices, the emotional impact of seeing the house in the first 30 seconds often determines which home is purchased. If your house is purchased one, two or six months earlier it will save thousands and in some cases tens of thousands of dollars in staging, mortgage and maintenance costs as a home sits on the market, not to mention the cost of needing to discount the price as it earns the reputation of being a "slow-seller."

This last part of the equation (How easy is it for a buyer to imagine landscaping the area in question) provides the potential for the most profit per dollar invested. If you have an area of your landscape or home that causes anxiety and uncertainty about how to address it for the typical buyer, fixing it will often increase the value of your home significantly more than the cost of doing so.

This is particularly the case when a problem can be fixed in a creatively cost-effective and attractive way that the average buyer could not have imagined. Terracing and planting an intimidating slope might be one example of this. Reducing the hazard from a precariously placed tree above the house would be another. Creatively leveling an area for lawn in a family house with steep hills might be a third. Having a creative, practical designer on your team to brainstorm in this area can be priceless.

This does not mean that if you have a landscape that is already nicer than most in your neighborhood that investing more money in it purely for your own pleasure will have NO real-estate return on investment. It merely means that either a smaller percentage of buyers will be willing to buy your house for the price you want, which means it may take longer to find someone willing to pay your price. Or if you want to sell quickly you may only get fifty, sixty or seventy cents on the dollar rather than one to three dollars of return for each dollar you invest.

Another thing to consider that affects real-estate value includes creating a landscape that is consistent with the profile of the typical buyer for your home. If you have a three to five bedroom house the typical buyer will have children and want some level lawn for their kids to play on. Putting that lawn in might make the difference between your house being purchased quickly by such a family, who could not imagine creating an area for lawn on a hillside themselves. Similarly, if your home fits the profile of a second home for retirees, low maintenance and landscape simplicity might be selling points.

Managing Your Cash-Flow

The following are simple ways to help your cash flow:

One of the most important tools in managing cash-flow is doing a project in stages. Stages can take several forms.

- One is to install areas incrementally, such as doing the front garden and then the back.

- Another way may be a more complex strategy, such as doing all the walls in the entire landscape but initially planting the beds with wildflowers and planting the permanent plants with their irrigation, soil prep and mulch at a later date. This approach allows you to take advantage of certain efficiencies in scale.

- Other strategies include adding things such as lighting and water features as a last stage.

Perhaps the most important consideration in managing your cash-flow is your overall budget for the project. If your overall project budget is $60,000.00 and you want to start with the front yard, you may need to come up with $30,000.00 for stage one. If on the other hand your total project budget is half that, stage one might be closer to $15,000.00. This chapter dove-tails with the next chapter on how to save money, where you can learn ways of reducing your total project cost.

There is usually a natural tension between saving the most money RIGHT NOW and saving the most money long-term. For example, breaking a project into stages can add to overall project costs as follows:

- When hiring a landscape company for your installation it is typically more efficient to for them to install an overall landscape at one time garden vs. doing it in stages. I and other landscape companies may offer an "efficiency discount" of around 10% for larger projects done all at once. This savings is lost when breaking a project into stages.

- In addition to this, some designs are a lot more expensive to install in stages for practical reasons. In the example of doing a front and back garden separately, if both gardens require the use of an excavator and several types of materials delivered, it could be that partial truckloads are brought to the property that require full delivery charges. Or lets imagine that we grade the front and back gardens simultaneously but only plant the front garden in year one. The back-garden will grow full of weeds, which may require hundreds or thousands of dollars to strip off again in order to avoid additional maintenance costs that come from tilling weeds into the soil before planting.

- There is also inflation to consider. This typically ranges between 2-7% per year. Inflation in a landscape comes in three areas that function independently of one another. Any one or all three can go up in a given year:

  o Increased labor costs.

  o Increased material costs.

  o Increased permit, code restrictions, environmental management, engineering requirements and other costs. Of the three, this is the most unrelenting.

There are good reasons for doing things in stages, even if that means paying more overall. Many of these are emotional reasons, combined with uncertainty about the future. Since gardens are intended to support quality of life it can be far better to spend an extra 15% on a landscape done in stages if it means that you will feel 20% more relaxed and in control of your finances for two years, over doing everything at once and feeling over-extended.

However; if you are clear what you want to do and that you are going to do it, it is typically cheaper to do the entire project at one time. This has the added bonus of allowing you to enjoy your entire landscape for one to three more years, rather than waiting for parts of it to be complete.

How to Save Money!

In this section I will share several of the best ways to save money without compromising the quality and value of your project.

Creative design: One of the most important areas to save money is by getting creative with the design. If you can come up with two great designs and one requires half the work/cost to install, you will realize an instant and long-term savings. The bigger the project the more valuable it is to examine several ways to achieve your goals, along with each of their separate costs. Just one good idea can save tens of thousands of dollars on a larger project.

Doing it yourself: Once you have a good design there are at typically some aspects of it that you can do yourself. As labor represents about half of any project cost, anything you can do well is a great way to save money, providing it does not cost you more money in time off work and/or medical care in the event you take on a hard project without proper physical conditioning. This might include areas such as:

- Doing demolition work on the existing site before work begins.
- Planting plants in newly created beds.
- Adding drip irrigation to plants.
- Mulching the plants with bark.
- Installing low-voltage lights.

Shopping around: Getting multiple bids is another way to save money. There is almost always a cheaper contractor out there if you take the time to find them. While this may expose you to other risks that stem, for example, from hiring an unlicensed contractor that could come back to haunt you, it may be worth the risk to you to save hundreds or thousands of dollars. Even within the sub- group of quality, licensed landscape contractors there will be variations in the bids for several reasons:

- One contractor may have a lot more time than another and so offer a lower than normal price.

- One contractor may have a different installation technique that is more or less labor intensive than the other (this is an area that is very hard for anyone without a lot of experience to measure).

- One contractor may have leftover materials that can be used on the job that they want to get rid of and thus include in their bid at a discount.

- One contractor may pay their crew less money.

- One contractor may be a poor estimator and over or under-bid the job in a way that benefits you.

- One contractor may have higher overhead than another and pass those costs on to you.

Landscaping is often not an apples and apples comparison in the way that a house is. Unlike building a house, where there are clearer standards for how things are done, it can be best to look at a landscaper's prior work to see how words that look similar on paper can produce very different landscapes in quality and style.

Smaller plants: There is no stock I know of where you can get a guaranteed 100% return on investment per year. However, you get at least this guaranteed return on investment when you buy four inch plants instead of gallons, or gallons instead of five gallon plants. Here are two typical scenarios that illustrate the savings of smaller plants, using three hundred plants as an example, which is a typical number of plants for a small Marin garden:

- 300 X $4.00 for a typical four inch plant = $1,200.00 Planting each four inch plant might cost $2.00 for a total of $600.00 and a grand total of $1,800.00 for 300 installed four inch plants (not including soil prep, irrigation and mulch).

- 300 X $8.00 for a typical one gallon plant = $2,400.00 Planting each gallon might cost $4.00 for a total of $1,200.00 and a grand total of $3,600.00.

- 300 X $20.00 for a typical five gallon plant = $6,000.00 Planting each five gallon plant might cost $10.00 for a total of $3,000.00 and a grand total of $9,000.00

The incredible thing is that in many cases the five gallon plant is only eighteen months older than the four inch plant. In other words in a small garden you will be paying around $7,000.00 for the garden to look mature eighteen months faster. $7,000.00 is enough to install a small custom water-feature, upgrade plain concrete to stamped concrete, or put in a weather controlled smart irrigation controller and nice outdoor lighting for a small garden. In eighteen months the plants will fill in and you will never know the difference. But if you leave out a major hardscape feature you will either miss it forever or pay even more, thanks to staging and inflation costs, to put it in later.

Being Flexible: Being flexible allows you to take advantage of discounted opportunities in several areas.

- Nurseries often have plant specials on specific plants. Substituting these for some of the plants in your design can save you 50% on select plants.

- Craigslist or a friend may offer materials for free or a discount, reducing some material costs by 100%.

- Your landscape contractor may be able to give you a discount if you are flexible in such areas as: when they do the work or what types of materials are used. In the latter case they may have left-over material from another job and in the former if you are clear that saving money is more important than doing the work by a set time this gives them the opportunity to take profitable last-minute job opportunities, while coming back to your project when they are slow and making less money per hour but staying busy.

- Flexibility around timing also allows you to use the lowest bidder even if they are booked out six months before they can get to your job.

- If you are flexible about what you want it also allows your designer to come up with the design that requires the least amount of change to your existing site. For example, you can save money on your water bill by putting in drought tolerant plants. If on the other hand you spell out your favorite plants and many of them require high water there is no way to lower your water bill.

- If you want lawn but do not require a level lawn a design may be possible that avoids thousands of dollars in grading costs.

Soil Amendment: See the chapter on soil-amendment to learn how you can save thousands of dollars on the typical landscape by using the recommended approach rather than bringing in topsoil.

Permits for your Landscape

Finding out a comprehensive list of all landscape codes in straight-forward English, along with a list of required permits and fees is not easy. As preparation for this book I e-mailed the Marin Municipal Water District, every town and city and Marin County. It took an average of ten minutes per city to find their website and the right person to contact and the city of Mill Valley was the ONLY city to respond with any information. The other towns/cities either did not respond at all or wrote back to say they would respond shortly and never did! The Marin municipal water district never responded. If requests for a book are treated so cavalierly, imagine how you – a mere citizen- will be treated!

The most helpful response (and it was surprisingly helpful, as you will see) came two weeks later (several people were on vacation so my e-mail did not reach the right party for weeks) was from the county. I've included my letter from Curtis below as the most helpful guide to permitting issues in straight-forward English available, if you live in the un-incorporated areas of Marin.

This experience of having to work hard to access information is consistent as a statistic with my experience of dealing with government on all levels, with a few refreshing exceptions. Contacting a switch-board to ask a complex question, there is a 50% chance that you will be sent to the wrong department or given erroneous information. This happens in big institutions on all levels. There is often only a few people in local government that know the answer to a complex question it takes some doing to find out who those people are without pissing everyone else in the office off. It's not uncommon for someone who is not qualified to answer a question to answer it anyway and then feel offended when you ask to speak to someone who is more qualified.

Once you find the person or people who really know how all the departments work together and how the codes between various aspects intersect, it's often hard to get information in a useful format, such as: "Can you tell me a way to screen my high neighbor's window without getting a permit or with the minimum of hassle?" The question they want to answer is: "Do I need a permit for a six foot solid wood fence between here and here." And even there, one person may tell you one thing and another department says something else. Or if you need to go up eight feet to create privacy between you and your neighbor and want to know how the city or county would react to you raising your soil level two feet, building a two foot retaining wall and then building a six foot wall on top of that (creating your eight feet of total screen) you may or may not get a straight and cooperative answer.

There are several reasons for this. These are not elective officials. Creative thinkers often don't feel drawn to bureaucratic positions. Codes are often complex and many staffers don't know them well and don't want to admit ignorance or bother to look something up. They are not rewarded by saying "yes" but may be reprimanded for telling you something is OK that someone else in the department finds is in violation of a code. The solution to all of this that is most commonly suggested is: draw it all up and submit it for review. However, the time you need the information is BEFORE you develop your design so you can design things in a way that avoids the very hassle of having to submit many plans for review. It can be quite frustrating when you realize how much time and money is wasted going about things backwards.

I share all of this so that you have some sense of what to expect and so that you don't take any of it personally. On the bright side, here is the very helpful letter from the county that I mentioned:

Hi Dane,

A property owner should first contact their local water provider (e.g. Marin Municipal Water District, North Marin Water District, etc.) prior to preparing landscaping plans. As of January 1, 2010, local water districts are responsible for implementing the "Model Water Efficient Landscape Ordinance" enacted by the State of California. Starting with your local water district will ensure that you are in compliance with these water conservation requirements.

Another worthwhile agency to check in with before getting too far along in planning a landscaping project is the local fire department. The Marin County Fire Department often requires a "Vegetation Management Plan" (VMP) to ensure the project does not add to the potential fire hazards. The requirements for a VMP can be found at this link: http://www.xmrfire.org/mrn/Prevention%20Documents/MCFD%20VMP%20Standard_REV_3.pdf

The "Homeowner's Guide to Fire Safe Practices" can be found here: http://www.xmrfire.org/mrn/Prevention%20Documents/Marin%20landscape%20brochureREV2.pdf

Projects that are located within one hundred feet of a watercourse or wetlands area should take special measures to prevent runoff and pollution. For more information about techniques to minimize or prevent storm water runoff and pollution, please refer to http://mcstoppp.org/

For properties located within the unincorporated areas of Marin County, please contact the Marin County Planning Department at (415) 499-6269 for information about fencing, retaining walls, pergolas, trellises, and other design features commonly found in yards. Generally speaking, fences cannot exceed six feet in height and the top two feet of a fence must be at least 50% open. Retaining walls should not exceed a height of four feet. If a retaining wall needs to be taller than four feet, it is recommended that the retaining wall is broken into four-foot tall segments with at least two feet of separation between walls to allow for screening landscaping.

Finally, property owners should be aware that removal of certain types and sizes of trees may require a tree removal permit. Please refer to Chapter 22.27 of the Marin County Development Code for more information.

That is probably about as brief as I can keep it. I hope this is enough information to be useful to you. If you have any questions, feel free to contact me.

Regards,

Curtis Havel

Senior Planner
Marin County Community Development Agency
3501 Civic Center Drive, Room 308
San Rafael, CA 94903
(415) 507-2755
(415) 499-7880 (fax)

This is another helpful letter form the city of Mill Valley.

Hi Dane,

Thank you for the opportunity to provide information from the City of Mill Valley for your new book. The City does not have codified landscape requirements, except for those restrictions related to fire prevention as part of the Wild land Urban Interface (WUI) code. The link on the City's website to that information is at:

http://www.cityofmillvalley.org/Index.aspx?page=433

The City also has residential design guidelines that address landscaping. They can be found at:

http://www.cityofmillvalley.org/Index.aspx?page=747

Landscaped areas over a specified threshold also must be reviewed and approved by the Marin Municipal Water District to insure that they meet a required water budget.

If you have any other questions, please feel free to contact me.

Mike Moore
Planning & Building Director
City of Mill Valley
26 Corte Madera Avenue
Mill Valley, CA 94941
Ph: 415-388-4033 x 107
E-mail: mmoore@cityofmillvalley.org

In my opinion your very best strategy, when possible is to avoid designing a project that requires permits of any kind, when feasible. Avoiding the need for permits by designing with that intention will typically save you between 30-300% in not only money but time and hassle.

Here are some of the approaches I use when designing a landscape to avoid the need for a permit:

- Know the property lines and the easements. Then avoid major structural activity, such as fences, walls and sheds within any easements or outside the property line.
- Build walls under 4' high and in such a way that they are not retaining a major slope. This typically results in a decorative wall rather than a retaining wall classification.
- Build fences 6' high or less.
- Do not grade more than twenty yards of soil at a time.

- Do not cut more than three major trees down at a time and do not cut down oak trees with more than a 6" diameter.
- Keep dumpsters off the street and on the property.
- Avoid upsetting the neighbors or freaking them out by doing large projects in stages.
- Avoid landscaping within 25' of any wetland/stream.
- Do not install permanent structures bigger than 120 square feet.
- Do not work on weekends and be done by 6pm.
- Avoid adjustments to sewer lines or bring in a plumber.
- Avoid major structural changes to decks so that they can be worked with as a repair that does not require a structural engineer.
- Make minimal structural changes to steep slopes.
- Remove as much impervious surface area as you add.
- Use low-voltage landscape lighting rather than high voltage lighting.

I also want to point out a gray area to illustrate a principle that is at play when it comes to permits. It's not something I've ever seen written down anywhere but it is at work in practice all the time.

Depending on your location, you may or may not be required to submit a "planting plan" for a major landscape project. But does this mean that you will be taken to task for planting one daisy? And then, a year later, another daisy? You may be required to get a grading permit to move more than twenty yards of material. Does this mean that if you go out with your wheelbarrow and move a few wheelbarrows of dirt a day that someone is going to complain that you don't have a grading permit? You may be required to get a permit to stabilize your slope. But if you go out and plant some ivy or bamboo on it, one plant at a time, will that trigger a permit requirement? You may be required to get a deck-repair permit. Does this mean that if you go out and replace one board on the deck this month and next month another board that an official will be upset if they notice the new board?

In other words, if you do things on a big enough scale all at once almost EVERYTHING requires a permit. If you do small things slowly almost NOTHING in landscaping requires a permit. You still can't build ten foot fences, however slowly. But if you and your neighbor both agree that you want a ten foot fence between you and you are prepared to lower it or remove it when one of you sells if the new owner wishes it, then in most cases it will not be an issue, as long as it does not block another neighbors view.

You will not typically run into problems if you do quality work and knowledgeably act with consideration for all involved, including your neighbors. I will often approach neighbors in the design-stage in order to understand any concerns they may have prior to finalizing or installing a landscape. This has a number of side-benefits, including the potential for cost-sharing.

In most cases the penalty for doing something without a permit is double the normal permit fees. In addition you may or may not be required to:

- Provide a soils report supporting the work you have done.
- Provide a structural engineer's report supporting the work you have done.
- Redo your project or make modifications to conform to the above and to code.

Be aware that it is ultimately the home-owners responsibility to obtain any needed permits. If you are having work done and want to make sure that it has a permit if needed, you will need to take your plans to your city/town and perhaps the county as well. The permit fee may be in the range of 10-20% of the project cost. Engineering reports usually start on the low end at $1,000 and don't normally exceed $10,000.00 for landscape-related work.

However, keep in mind that bringing in engineers can increase project costs in much more significant ways than simply paying for their report. A professionally installed dry stack stone wall that is three feet high and costs $7,000.00 might become a $15,000.00 wall at four feet six inches if it is classified as a retaining wall, requiring a permit, soils report and structural engineer. For that matter, if the structural engineer has trouble computing the load-bearing capacity of hand-laid dry stack stone they may ask you to switch materials to something less attractive and durable, such as wood or, in some cases, poured cement with a stone finish and additional drainage, bringing the project cost to $25,000.00. This would be a great example of where a design calling for one three foot wall and another two foot wall would save significant time, money and hassle, and probably look better.

Note: It is in areas such as this that the big money is saved or wasted on a landscape project. A good designer will inform you of the pros and cons of choices like this and how they affect your costs as part of the design process.

Integrating Landscaping with Your Custom Home or Remodel

If you are building a new home or doing a major remodel affecting the exterior of your home, I have great news! Using some very simple and uncommon techniques you can save up to 30% of the cost of your landscape while enhancing the functional and aesthetic value of your home!

Integrating landscaping with your home-building process is one of those things that is great for the consumer but rarely happens because it is outside of the normal job description of your typical builder, architect, realtor or landscaper. When I had trouble convincing builders, architects and home-owners of the benefit of developing an integrated home and landscape design I met with resistance on all fronts. So I decided to make a showcase. Here are the results:

- I was able to buy a very nice lot for half price because most people could not figure out how to build on it.
- I hired an architect to develop a house-design consistent with the house footprint I had painted out on site and roughly sketched, based on what would work as an integrated house and landscape.
- By working out ALL the details of both the house and landscape PRIOR to beginning the project I was able to PREPARE for my builder and hand him:
  o Permitted drawings.
  o A foundation cut that was ready to pour.
  o Driveway cut in with stone walls already in place, making parking easier.
  o A list of all lighting, appliance and plumbing fixtures, along with their prices and where to find them.

- o   A list of all paint colors.
- o   A septic system already installed with all drainage and utilities stubbed off.
- o   All soil mulched and level around the construction envelope.
- This in turn led my builder to give me a VERY good price for the job. Why? A builder's biggest hassle is weather, running into a buried stump while putting in a driveway, trying to find the water line or dealing with a client that is delaying the schedule with indecision or last minute changes that cost everyone money. Not to mention being asked to give a bid on something that does not yet have a permit, which means waiting AND the probability that the city or county will requires some change that will affect the cost. What I had given him was the easiest house and client relationship he had ever had. And as a result he could easily deliver on the ONLY things I made him promise: 1) there would be NO additions to the price and 2) it would be done ON TIME.
- Finally, I sold the completed home for FULL PRICE ABOVE APPRAISED VALUE (some appraisers do not value landscapes but buyers will always go for what they want the most) in a SLOW real estate market. The buyer (who I talked with) told me simply that it was the nicest integrated home/landscape on the market in her price range.
- I saved 30% overall and more in specific areas of landscaping by doing the techniques I'm going to share with you below!

To explain how this is possible, I'll begin by sharing how things normally happen on a construction project. A piece of land is bought with minimal consideration for the cost of landscaping it. The home is built with the builder/architect giving minimal or no thought to the landscape design. This is particularly true if there is no Architect involved and a builder and client work from a set of purchased plans.

If they do give some thought to the landscape it is often not consistent with what the home-owner ultimately does. As a result when I get called in to design and build a landscape I need to commonly fix a number of problems:

- Drains are not where they need to be.
- Grading has to be redone.
- The siding/foundation profile does not match the ultimate landscape design well.
- The water line has to be dug up again for irrigation connection.
- New electrical lines/outlets need to be added.
- Materials need to be hauled to the back of the house by hand rather than utilizing the heavy machinery that was onsite as part of home- construction.
- Dump trucks can't drop materials easily on newly poured driveways so the cost of materials goes up to have them put into pallets and brought in by forklift.
- Concrete has already been poured in ways that are not consistent with an ideal landscape plan, which means it needs to be re-done or worked with as a compromise.
- Some trees have been removed that would have added to the landscape design and lowered costs.
- Trenches need to be re-dug to lay electrical and irrigation lines when these could have been easily added to the construction trenches at half the cost.

These and other problem areas are ALL areas you can save money by planning ahead! By developing a well-thought-out landscape plan BEFORE you build you can realize the following savings AND make things easier for the builder:

- Spread two inches bark on all bare soil at the beginning of construction. This will prevent mud in the house, keep tools and building materials clean and bio-degrade into good organic matter that can be tilled in prior to planting.

- Deliver any heavy materials, such as topsoil and stone to remote portions of the property before the house foundation blocks access to those areas, saving thousands in labor costs.
- Show your builder the landscape plans so that the grading, drainage and utility work is done compatibly with the plan and save thousands of dollars.
- Have the builder install any electrical lines needed for the landscape while doing the electrical work for the house. This will save an average of $1,500.00
- Have the builder lay PVC irrigation lines in all utility trenches and stub this off. This will save an average of $1,000.00 in labor.
- Have the builder lay empty pipe at least 1" thick under all poured concrete. This will save an average of $500.00 when it comes time for low voltage lighting, drip lines etc.
- Have the builder create an irrigation shut off valve for easy connection later. This costs $50.00 and saves $400.00 digging up the house line. It also means your main water won't be shut off during landscaping.
- If you like a native look, avoid cutting down as much as possible of the native habitat. This can save you as much as $30,000.00 in replanting costs (One client spent $100,000.00 replanting native plants cut down or bulldozed by a careless builder who did not bother to ask what style of landscape that client wanted.)
- Have the builder place switches in the house that will control such things as landscape lighting, water-falls and pond lights. This can save around $500.00 over doing it later.
- Utilize construction equipment to place any large rocks you may want to feature. This will save an average of $500.00 over bringing in equipment later.

- Some construction waste can be recycled for sheds, retaining walls and other garden projects, helping the environment at a savings.
- Have your contractor work closely with you or the landscaper to grade the area before removing any heavy equipment. This might include pulling out stumps, digging holes for ponds, or flattening an area out for lawn with a cut for a retaining wall. This will save you an average of $1,200.00 and possibly a lot more if it is hard to get equipment on site.

Because the savings can be so staggeringly huge and this is not an area that you, your architect or builder may be familiar with, this is one area where spending the one to two thousand dollars it may take to bring out a good landscape designer will really pay off. I've listed some of the ways you can save money but that is not necessarily the biggest reason to think about your landscape PRIOR to and during construction. In many cases a little forethought can result in a SIGNIFICANTLY nicer landscape at no extra cost – simply by having an idea BEFORE parts of the house are built that could easily fit with the landscape.

How I built a nicer house for less: For those of you are interested in one example of a step-by step approach that integrates landscaping intelligently into a construction process and simultaneously minimizes the risk of cost-overruns, here is how I went about building the house I referred to earlier:

- I chose a lot bordering a stream, which has a 100' setback with a large plot of forested land behind me. This made building a large house unfeasible but insured ongoing privacy.
- I used spray-paint on the lot to roughly develop a house landscape concept before making an offer on the land.
- I developed a 1200 square feet design, and placed it as far from the stream as was feasible, to insure county

approval, which would require a waiver from the 100' stream setback.

- I met with the county PRIOR to submitting plans or buying the land (the land had been sitting for sale for years since people could not figure out how to build on it and it seemed risky to them so I had plenty of time) and verified that my plan would almost certainly be approved.
- I wrote a letter of intent to the land-owner (against my real-estate agent's advice) offering to buy the land in any one of three ways, including an all-cash price for the least amount of money, a one year note for slightly more and a lease-option for a bit more than that. All prices were less than the lot-owner had paid for the property ten years before (as I said, it was a stagnant market) and about half of appraised value.
- The land-owner accepted option two, which called on me to give them 15%, down with the balance due within 18 months.
- I then set to work (without any hurry) to prepare the site for construction:
  - I hired a good septic designer/installer to give me a bid and work with me to put the septic system to the far rear of the property. Based on my rough design I told them how deep to bury the septic tanks.
  - I then hired a logger to only take out the trees needed for the septic system to be installed and the house and landscape to be built. I designed the house and landscape to work around most of the trees staying by insuring that the grade would not change around their roots. I hired a logger instead of doing this work myself because he was able to take the removed trees to a sawmill and

deduct that from my bid, while disposing of the trees.

o I then moved on site with my equipment and cut out the driveway, created additional guest-parking by cutting into the slope and building four foot stone walls that held the area up.

o At this point I brought the septic installer in to do his work, having provided him with easy access for his dump-trucks to get near the drainfield.

o I again spray-painted the house footprint on the ground, this time adding windows, doors, room layouts and such so I could see what my views would be and how things would feel. As much as possible, I tried to pretend that the house was already built so I could see what kind of home I would want to live in.

o I then went to the architect, brought him on site, asked him about different finishing details and how they affected costs. I then gave him a list of requested finishing details I wanted (these specs determine around 30% of the cost). I asked him for a maximum budget, working hourly, to design and engineer a set of plans based on my floor plan and I showed him my landscape ideas so he would know how to design the foundation and siding profiles. When we agreed on that, I asked to be included in the process by being notified at three different stages so that I could review the drawing before the next step of drawings were done.

o When these plans were finished I brought them to the county.

o Because I was acting as a general contractor and had already done much of the site work, the permit fees were slightly lower, based on a % of construction costs. I also saved paying my builder his markup on site work and I saved paying an architect his markup on everything, since the architect was not managing the project. Right here I saved 20% on the whole project, while simultaneously getting more of what I wanted.

- When the plans were approved by the county, I asked the builder I wanted to work with for a list of EVERY single decision he would need from me throughout the project in a written document.
- I then proceeded to answer every question up-front, including which fixtures would go where and gave him all of that. He had previously given me a bid with allowances. Now he gave me a set fixed price for everything.
- I accepted the price, which included me digging out the foundation cut for him so that he could form it up and pour it. We did this together, so that the foundation was just the way he wanted it.
- While the concrete was hardening I put in all the footing drains, gutter drains and irrigation pipe around the house and out to the street.
- I dug the trenches in such a way that I also created a trench for the main water line, which I stubbed off for the builder near the house.
- I then did touch up grading around the house and had tree-trimming companies bring me truckloads of free wood-chips to spread on all exposed soil on site. This minimized the mud for my builder AND provided organic matter and protection for the soil.
- I then disappeared completely for four months. There was nothing else for me to do. I drove by once or twice during this time but no meetings were required. The

builder had everything he needed to do the job well. All of our agreement was in writing and there were no variables. This was GREAT for the builder and equally great for me. No more last minute decisions and hassles. No worry. No cost overruns. Absolutely NOTHING but getting on with my life until the house was built.

- At the end, I came back to do the rest of the landscaping.
- I asked my neighbor if I could landscape a bit of her undeveloped property in a way that would make my land look bigger and improve the first impression of my house. She said "yes" and for and extra $3,000.00 I increased the appeal of my approach by 30%, creating good-will at the same time.

It's valuable to remember that you are not buying a house plus a landscape (this is the way things are often purchased) but a well-integrated home that is affordable, enjoyable and easy to live in. I've talked about the financial savings in some of the more common areas. These also translate into ecological savings. Having to tear up a gutter drain the builder has just installed and lay a new deeper line because the soil is regarded wastes petroleum, as well as money. Having to pay to dig up a water line to connect irrigation is money that could be spent on charity, your landscape.

This idea is commonly utilized by developers but very rarely by custom home-owners. It is one of the most exciting opportunities you have to create a lot more for less in this entire book. If you are not building but have a friend who is, please do them a favor and show them this chapter BEFORE they build! It is not uncommon for marriages to go through quite a strain in the building process so you may be helping them with something much more important than a home.

How Much Will it Cost?

It is not at all uncommon for me to be asked within five minutes of meeting a possible client: "Can you give me a rough idea about how much this will all cost?" This tells me that the potential client does not understand how important their role is in determining what the costs will be. At that point I know little or nothing about the person asking the question so I have no basis for giving an answer. If you are someone who wants to know how much your project will cost before you develop a detailed design, the following example may help you get a better feeling for ALL the costs involved in a landscape project and what generates them.

First, a landscape costs more than just the amount of money in a contract. Its costs can be broken down into:

- Money up front.

- Total long-term cost of installation and redoing things.

- Ongoing money for maintenance.

- Time spent organizing, designing and installing the landscape.

- Energy, hassle and disruption to your life.

The more energy is spent in any one of these categories the less needs to be spent in the others. For example, if you spend more money up-front with the goal of lowering maintenance then you need to spend less money on ongoing maintenance. If you are willing to spend more time organizing and planning you often spend less time installing. And if you focus on avoiding hassle and disruption to your lifestyle you typically spend more money to work with a contractor known for reliability and service. If you buy cheap materials now you will spend more in maintenance and possibly redoing things later. Finally, if you spend more time doing some of the installation yourself you will spend less money.

None of these costs are black and white. Each exists on a gray-scale and the trick is finding the right point on the dial for each of these costs.

Let's look at a practical example of a hillside above a retaining wall that is landscaped differently in two scenarios: "How much will it cost?"

Scenario One:

- Client consults with a designer and spends $400.00 developing a low-cost action plan for the slope using flags to mark plants, video and client notes to avoid the cost of scale drawings.

- Client orders five yards of chicken compost from American soils for $300.00 and spreads this two inches thick on the slope.

- Client buys a mini tiller (not available for rent) at Home Depot for $400.00 and tills this into the slope, selling the tiller on Craig's list for $200.00 for a net $200.00 cost.

- Client buys $400.00 in the form of 45 one gallon plants and 20 4" plants from Home Depot. Plants have been carefully chosen by designer to be deer resistant (nothing is deer proof) and drought tolerant once established. Most have dense evergreen foliage and are at least 18" tall so that they block weeds year-round.

- Client contacts local arborists and arranges for one to dump 30yards of wood chips for FREE. Client spreads these 3-4" thick on the slope.

- Client hand waters these well and then puts a stake in the ground at the top of the slope where they mount a rotating sprinkler attached to a hose. This is attached to a battery operated timer and attaches to a hose bib for a grand total of $89.00

- Within three years the plants have filled in densely and require only four hours of maintenance a year. A few watering's in July and August help but are not required.

- **Grand total for all: $1,389.00**

Scenario Two:

- Client consults with a landscape designer to develop a detailed drawing and design for the slope: $1,300.00

- Client is concerned about the structural stability of the slope so a soils engineer is consulted prior to beginning the design: $1,500.00

- Engineer recommends several basic approaches that the client decides to have done: $3,400.00

- Client wants to terrace the slope somewhat and place several large decorative boulders on it as focal points: $8,200.00

- Client requests outdoor lighting be installed and opts for high-grade cast bronze fixtures controlled both by a timer and a remote override: $3,100.00

- Client requests an instant effect so forty 5-15 gallon plants are brought in and planted: $4,800.00

- Decorative bark is spread on the whole area: $3,000.00

- Plants need regular watering and a custom drip irrigation system is installed for them: $2,100

- **Total cost: $27,400**

Scenario two without getting at all outrageous is almost TWENTY times more expensive than scenario one. When they are all done in five years they don't look that different from one another either! One has lights and slightly bigger plants and that's about it. But in the first case the client focused on saving money and did all the work and in the second case the client saved time, hassle and bought themselves added re-assurance and an instant effect. They paid $26,011.00 more for those luxuries.

In other words MOST of the cost depends on YOU! Before I can advise a client on costs I look at all their answers to the detailed questionnaire included in this book. In particular I pay attention to their answers to:

- Do things have to be perfect or adequate to get the job done?

- How much money do you want to spend overall?

- How much money do you want to spend now?

- Do you want to participate in any of the work? If so how many hours are you willing to invest? What can you do?

- How much money are you willing to spend in maintenance to get the landscape you want?

- Is stress a high factor in your life and does it make sense to pay more money to lower the stress of a project?

- How long are you willing to wait before your landscape feels mature?

- Are you willing to limit your plant list to hardy low-maintenance plants?

- What are you passionate about including in your landscape?

When I understand my clients in ALL of these areas I can tell them exactly how much something will cost because I design things to reflect their budget and values.

When one landscaper says your garden will cost about $10,000.00 and another says it will cost about $5,000.00 it is probably not the same landscape at all. Before things are spelled out in detail it simply means that one landscaper is guessing you will make one set of decisions and the other is guessing you will make another set of decisions. NEITHER one actually knows what you will decide so both are likely to be wrong. It is your decisions that will determine the cost. Only when you have a detailed design and two separate bids AND have seen the quality levels of the two contractors on prior work can you gain accurate information about which estimate or bid provides you with the most value.

And it may not be the cheapest bid that gives you personally the most value. If you get irritated when you need to repeat yourself and want someone you can relate to and you have a good rapport with the more expensive contractor, you may be much happier taking their bid. Or perhaps you don't like the cheaper contractor but you really like fine craftsmanship and the cheaper contractor does fabulous work but has a hard time getting clients because they are rude and late so they compete on price. You may feel happier putting up with rude and late and really enjoying the quality work for years to come.

Maximizing Functional Property Potential

If you are someone who likes to see that all of your land is utilized well, creating an overall design that efficiently utilizes each asset and area will be important. Your property is unique and so is the way you live, but here are a few things you can consider:

- Adding a solar station or a vegetable garden in particularly sunny areas.

- Adding a mini wind-mill in areas with a steady breeze.

- Building small road or trail to provide access to steep unused areas of your land.

- Terracing steep hillsides to plant and enjoy.

- Catching and storing rain-water for back-up irrigation in either underground containers or a pond.

- Examining all the ways you want to use a space before building it and planning ahead if doing the project in stages.

  o A lawn area can double as a volley ball court if it is designed to be big enough.

  o Decks can be built big enough to include space for a herb-garden or pots in the winter.

  o Trenches for one utility can include conduit in them so other utilities can be pulled through at a later time.

Designing to Lower Your Maintenance

Maintenance is important for two reasons:

- Over time it is probable that you will spend more time and money maintaining your landscape than you did installing it.
- If you design a garden that is too time-consuming or expensive to maintain your efforts to create a beautiful garden are wasted.

Maintenance comes in six categories:

- Watering
- Pruning and dead-heading flowers
- Weeding
- Replacing plants
- Replacing hardscape materials
- Mowing

What follows are basic strategies for lowering maintenance in each of these areas.

Watering:

- Install a reliable irrigation system using a smart timer.
- Plant plants that require little or no water.
- Mulch and amend soil well to retain water.
- Utilize hardscapes with minimal plantings.
- Using synthetic turf eliminates the need to water lawns.

Pruning and dead-heading flowers:

- Pick plants that grow to their desired size and then stop.
- Pick plants that grow slowly.

- Pick darker colored smaller flowers that are less noticeable when not deadheaded.

Weeding:

- Always mulch planting areas with at least two inches of infertile, insulating material.
- Use plants that are dense, evergreen, and at least one foot tall to block out weeds beneath them.
- Plant spreading plants meeting the above criteria that grow together in a dense mat, reducing the need for mulching.

Replacing plants:

- Pick long-lasting plants.
- Avoid annuals.

Replacing/refinishing hardscape materials:

- Sandstone tends to leach its color and wear away, requiring regular pressure washing and sealers. Avoid this and go with other flagstones and wall-facings, such as Three River's flagstone.
- Bamboo lattice/trellis etc. tends to deteriorate in about five years. Cast iron, aluminum or hardwood lasts a lot longer.
- Cheap low-voltage lighting fixtures often lose their patina and fall apart after 3-5 years. Get better quality.
- Use LED bulbs in low voltage fixtures and they will last two to ten times longer than other bulb options.
- Using Trex Deck and similar products reduces the need for ongoing staining/treatment of decking material and can last longer than wood.
- Using a one-coat penetrating stain for wood decking is half the work to apply both the first and second time compared with painting.

- Applying a high-gloss thick sealer on stone patios right after construction makes them easier to clean and preserves the color and stone.
- In most cases avoiding landscape fabric will save time in the long run.

Mowing:

- Using synthetic turf will eliminate the need for mowing. However it will often require adjustments every few years to compensate for minor settling in some areas. Leaves that fall on the top will require d raking/vacuuming.
- Using an electric, battery operated mower for small lawns may speed things up and save time getting gas for a can.
- Installing a 6" lawn border in brick, flush stone, or poured concrete will stop weeds growing into beds and provide a surface for the mower wheel to run along that eliminates the need for edging.
- In general, when all things are taken into account, it does not typically lower maintenance to swap out lawn for plantings. Replacing plants every five to ten years, mulching, weeding and the work involved in swapping them out typically offsets any savings in mowing twice a month.
- Ironically, since small water-features are often relatively high maintenance, a LARGE water feature can sometimes be lower maintenance than a lawn and even consume less water. A water feature that is lower maintenance than lawn will typically need to be at least four hundred square feet and at least four feet deep.

Landscaping Your Septic or Sewer System

The vast majority of Marin is connected directly with a municipal sewer system. Most of the time this means that a four inch sewer pipe goes underground from the low point in the house to a pipe buried in the street. From there it flows to a sewer treatment plant. To landscape a home with this set-up involves one of three strategies:

- As the landscape is graded, avoid cutting into this sewer pipe and make sure that any clean-out valves for this pipe have easy access.
- If the existing sewer pipe (typically called a "sewer line") precludes an important adjustment in the grade the sewer pipe can be cut up hill from the grade change and redirected, while still retaining enough of an angle that sewage will continue to travel down it using gravity. The minimum pitch of a pipe relying on natural gravity for flow is commonly considered to be two inches per ten feet. What this means is that in a twenty foot section of pipe the lower end would need to be AT LEAST four inches lower than the upper end, and preferably several times that amount.
- If there is not enough slope on your site to do the second option you can install a septic tank and pump. The sewage flows from the house to the tank using gravity and from there is pumped in whatever way you wished to the nearest sewer connect point. This effectively allows you to change the grade however you want.

Older homes and homes spaced farther apart may have a septic system, rather than a sewer connection. In this case the treatment of all sewage liquids is done on site using a drainage dispersion field and microorganisms, with the solids being pumped out from time to time.

This section is added primarily for homes with a septic system to highlight an important fact: **Your landscape can significantly impact the health and life-span of your septic system for better or for worse.** I learned all about septic systems when I lived on Whidbey Island because everyone had them. It's been eight years since a client of mine has had a septic system and new designs are always being innovated. However, what I share here will apply to systems older than fifteen years and to many of the new designs.

A septic system has four parts:

- The septic pipe, similar to those with a sewer connection that leaves the house.
- The septic tank, that collects all sewage and then disperses the liquids.
- The drainage dispersement field (or drainfield) that takes the liquids produced by the house showers, baths, toilets, laundry and sinks and deposits it beneath the ground.

Each of these parts can be affected by landscaping:

- The septic pipe can be affected as you have already seen in the prior page.
- The septic tank is typically made of plastic or concrete. In either case heavy trucks or equipment can crack, break or collapse the tank. It is important to know where the tanks are prior to landscaping and avoid placing heavy weights over them.
- The drainage dispersement field relies on aerobic bacteria to digest the sewage liquid (commonly called effluent) so that it will not clog the soil pores, stop working and require a new drainfield dispersement field to be

installed. As installing a new tank or drainfield can be a MAJOR expense, ranging from $6,000-$150,000 depending on many factors AND require you to tear up parts of your property or existing landscape, this is important to avoid.

Its important to realize that landscapers receive no formal training (most home-owners don't either) on proper care for septic systems. What this typically means is that if you don't understand this information there is a good chance a mistake will be made and you won't know about it until it is too late.

The basic principle of drainage dispersement fields is that they need air to get to the aerobic bacteria in order to keep the effluent from turning into a sticky slime that quickly leads to the need for a new drainage dispersement field. Most fields consist of trenches filled with gravel and 4" pipes with holes in them that evenly distribute the effluent over the entire length of the trench. The pipes are typically within the first 18" so that air can reach them. To avoid damaging your drainage dispersement field you need to:

- Not drive heavy equipment or trucks over them in ways that may either break the pipes or compact the soil.
- Landscape in a way that supports easy oxygen flow to the field. The very best planting over a drainfield is typically grass with little or no irrigation.

Landscaping that can damage a drainage dispersement field includes:

- Pouring concrete over all or part of it.
- Putting black plastic over all or part of it.
- Mulching the area with micro-bark more than 1" thick.
- Laying bricks or solid stone in mortar.
- Adding additional soil – particularly heavy soil.

- Irrigating – the more water used the worse off the field is.
- Compacting the soil over the field.
- Fencing with posts damaging the pipes.
- Putting in a water feature over the field.
- Running drainage pipes through the field.
- Having gutter pipes deposit water over the field.

The best thing to do if you have a drainfield is to examine the design, physically locate the various parts, learn about its operating parameters and then develop a landscape plan that will enhance the life of your system. Working creatively, it is possible to bend all of these rules in a way that has a net-positive impact on the entire system but allows you to create the landscape you want. If you feel uncertain and need more ideas or re-assurance, this is a great area to ask for help from a knowledgeable professional that is either a landscaper who understands septic systems or a septic installer that has some interest in landscaping.

Part Two:

The Design Process

What Makes a Design Great?

The first thing to realize is that a great design for YOUR garden is absolutely impossible without YOU! What makes a design great is how well it responds to your personal needs, preferences and values. A great design begins with you clarifying your very personal preferences, values and goals. Once these are established good design is a process of evaluating all of the options available to you to find the one option that takes you the closest to your goals, preferences and values within your budget.

Saying this another way, a $30,000.00 design that is visually stunning and high maintenance is not a great design for YOU if you prefer a low-key garden, low maintenance and have a budget of $20,000.00. The design that is best for you may never end up in a landscape magazine, but is still a GREAT design if it perfectly reflects your values, preferences, abilities and goals.

You are in fact the most important part of the design! There are a lot of "great" designs in sketch-books that will never get built because they either stray too far away from the preferences or the budget of the person they were intended for. These are not great designs for anyone but the designer who gets paid whether the designs are ever built or not.

Because you are the most important ingredient in the design process, we begin this section by examining your values, preferences and goals in two sections. The first will help you create your own definition of a successful project. The second is a series of landscape questions that will help you focus on what is most important to you in all areas of your landscape.

Defining Success

The first step in insuring your landscape's success is defining what success looks like for YOU. We all have different priorities and what is important to someone else may be quite different than what is important to you.

Here is a list of some of the more common priorities many people have in their landscape. To help you get clear on what is most important to you; rank each of the following goals using a 1-10 scale. For example, if maximizing real estate value is the bottom line you want to use to guide all your decisions you would give that a 10. If having the project done by a specific date is not at all important you would give that a zero.

- Maximizing Real-Estate Value.

- Saving Money NOW.

- Saving the most money long-term.

- Minimizing environmental impact.

- Having your project done on time.

- Minimizing construction impact on your lifestyle.

- Maintaining good neighbor relations.

- Maximizing functional property potential.

- Pleasing your personal taste.

- Good rapport with contractor.

- Exceptional workmanship.

- Doing everything legally and with permits.

- Being spontaneous and having fun with the project.

- Getting exercise and learning new skills as a challenge.

- Lowering your landscape's maintenance.

- Pleasing a partner/spouse.

- Creating personal space for relaxation and meditation.

- Other:

Your ranking of these areas will serve as a powerful compass as you make the hundreds of decisions that are involved in every landscape. So that you end up clearly focused, it is important to note your top **four** goals/values. These will become your guides as you examine your options and make up your mind.

This prioritization process is important because it will help you resolve the natural tensions that exist between such things as saving money NOW and saving money long-term. If saving money now is most important, one obvious choice is to do things in stages. However, stages can increase the total cost of a project (particularly when working with contractors) by eliminating efficiency savings that are natural when doing a large project at one time. Pleasing a partner may or may not correspond to maximizing real estate value and similar tensions may exist between most of these values so it's important to know what is most important to YOU!

Right after the next chapter on landscape questions you will learn how to use your rankings in this chapter and the answers from your questionnaire in a decision-making process that will help you create a great design. The prior section on landscape knowledge has already given you information about many of the strategies for achieving these goals. You will find more information in relating to some of these values in the last two section of this book.

Landscape Questions to Consider

Over the years I have observed many basic mistakes being made on projects. Some of these mistakes are so basic it is incredible! And yet they happen every day on typical landscape and construction projects. Why?

What it boils down to is that one or more key question did not get asked or answered and written down BEFORE the project was underway. Why does this happen? Client communication is not part of most landscape design training courses. Compounding this fact, most clients assume that a good designer will just know what is important to them without having to tell me. When these clients interact with designers who believe that they should understand their clients psychically there is a VERY high probability that something will not be clearly articulated and understood.

Another reason questions don't always get asked relates to the power-balance in a client/contractor relationship. Before you sign a contract, you have all the power and the contractor HAS to be reasonable on price. But once you sign the contract the power balance can shift in favor of the contractor. If in the middle of the project you realize "Oh my god! We forgot to run a conduit under the wall for the hot-tub we are planning next year. We need to add that in right away before the wall gets any higher..." then a change order is generated. And while you may not be happy about it, the contractor can charge a lot for those because it is now a monopoly relationship. And now that you have changed your mind in the middle of a project, they can side-step a commitment to have the work done on time.

That's why the first step of a great design is filling out the landscape questionnaire that follows. Its sole job is to see that ALL your needs are included in the design so that there are NO surprises, no cost overruns and no unnecessary delays! I give it to all my clients before making ANY design recommendations.

Not every question will apply to you. My goal in creating this questionnaire was to ask EVERY question that MIGHT relate to you and your site so that if you have anything you want to say to help me understand you that this happens BEFORE you risk making a costly mistake installing something that has been poorly thought out.

Even if you are going to do all of your own design and installation it is STILL important to write out your answers to this questionnaire because it will help you think clearly. I learned when I was designing and building my own custom home and landscape that it is not EASIER to design for myself but HARDER. I have helped hundreds of clients develop great ideas but when it came to my own design I found myself struggling to make up my mind without someone to bounce things off of. So I filled out my own questionnaire thoroughly and called a friend who was also a landscape designer to help me clarify my thoughts. I ended up with a great landscape that helped my home sell for full price above appraised value in a slow real estate market.

Note: Questions are spaced so you can fill in your answers in the book. You can also download a PDF of the latest version of the questionnaire from the design section of my website: www.MysticalLandscapes.com

Summarize what is most important to you about your Landscape:

Site/house Data:

1) If you are on a Septic System (in areas where there is no community sewer) do you know where the tank and drainfield is?

2) Are you aware of zoning restrictions, setbacks or other legal restrictions which might affect your landscape?
- Construction setbacks from streams/water?
- Setbacks from the street?
- Fencing restrictions?
- Neighborhood association guidelines?

3) Do you know where all utility cables are located?
- Gas line
- Water lines
- Sewer/Septic transfer line
- Power main and any auxiliary
- Phone

4) Do you have plans drawn to scale of the property and where the house sits on it? If so, please make a copy, white out any unnecessary information and make several copies of that to serve as draft sketching pads.

5) Do visible accurate stakes mark all property corners?

6) Might your neighbors be interested in helping you in any of the following ways:

- Sharing the cost of surveying, landscaping and/or fencing along the property line.
- Offering to pay for you to do something on your property that they want done, such as trimming a tree.

- Allowing you to bring materials or heavy equipment into your property through theirs if that is necessary.
- Giving you cuttings from their plants.
- Offering you advice about the animals in the neighborhood.

7) Are there hidden things not apparent?
- Buried stumps in areas
- Drainage problems in the winter
- Hard pan just below the surface in areas etc.

8) Which animals frequent the property: (Ask your neighbors if you are new to your home.)
- Deer
- Rabbits
- Other

9) Are there any existing features to the landscape you would like to leave unchanged (A tree you really like etc.)?

10) Are you planning structural changes to the house?
- Decks or patios
- Garage/ Remodel
- Other

11) Will the house be repainted the same colors? If not, which colors?

12) What is your water set up?
    a) Do you pay for it per unit?
    b) Is the hose-water filtered if you have an all-house water- filter system?
    c) Do you have good pressure?
    d) Are you on a community well?

Your Preferences:

1) Who in your family will be actively participating in the design process?

2) What atmosphere or style do you want your garden to have?

3) Do you prefer informal, semi-formal or very formal?

4) Would you like to attract any form of wildlife?
   1. Deer
   2. Rabbits
   3. Birds
   4. Butterflies

5) Would you like a water feature?

6) Is fragrance important to you?

7) Options for seasonal interest:
   a) The whole garden could be geared to be spectacular in 1-2 seasons
   b) Separate beds could be geared to be spectacular in different seasons
   c) Each area in the landscape could be quieter with something happening year round

8) Do you have favorite plants you want to include?

9) Are there plants you dislike?

10) Do you have color preferences?
   a) Colors you Dislike:
   b) Favorite Colors:

11) Do you have pictures that capture pieces of what you want in your garden? Notice what you like and dislike about these pictures.

12) Are there particular areas in the garden you want to make special?

13) How many years before you want your landscape to feel mature (this question refers to plant size mainly)?

14) Circle the materials and techniques you like and might want:

    a) Outdoor lighting:
- Are you interested in more expensive LED light bulbs where available? These last much longer, use less energy and are five times the cost of normal halogen bulbs.
- Would you prefer lower cost largely invisible fixtures with the focus being on the light or more expensive decorative features as a visual feature?
- Lights can be controlled at no extra charge by the timer that comes with the low voltage power supply or with an optional wireless switch or hardwired switch inside the house.

    b) Stone walls (local fieldstone or more expensive decorative rock)
    c) Natural stone Groupings
    d) Bark/ Chips (A 2-3" cover helps protect the soil from
    e) Groundcover
    f) Wood, Brick, Concrete, Pavers
    g) Gazebo
    h) Outside speakers and/or TV (where and controlled from where)
    i) Other:

14) Are there materials or techniques you want to avoid?

15) Would you like to create a designated space in your garden or home for meditation, relaxation and/or spiritual renewal?

Your Practical Needs:

1) Storage place for tools and bicycles?
2) A place to conceal the garbage cans?
3) Screening to block a particular view or create privacy from neighbors in areas?

4) A flat play area for games?
5) A wind screen?
6) An area you want to add more shade?
7) Space for vegetables or herbs?
8) A composting area for a heap or worm bin?
9) Site for a hot tub?
10) Easy wheel chair access? (If so, where to?)

11) How many cars do you want to comfortably park?
12) Are there other things (boats etc.) you plan to store on the site?
13) dog run/ animal shelter?
14) Do you want a fire pit?
15) Do have/ have plans for cat, dog or outside pets?
16) Will young children have unattended access to the landscape?
17) Do you need water, phone, propane, cable, a security system, intercoms, or electricity anywhere else on the site?

18) Do you want an automatic irrigation system?
   a) Drip or spray in bed areas?
   b) An onsite weather station linked to your irrigation controller or a new smart timer? (This has been

estimated to save about 30% of water and reduces maintenance.) water.

c) An optional remote for your irrigation controller.

Landscape Cost/Investments: (see chapters on cost/real estate value)

This includes anything outside the foundation footprint including garden sheds, driveway paving, drainage systems, outdoor lighting, forestry, trails etc.

1) Do you want a dollar for dollar return on investment in your landscape when you sell?

2) What do you want to pay for yearly maintenance once established:

3) All landscape related materials (includes annuals, bark etc.)$

- Paid help (if any): $

- How many hours do you want to spend maintaining your landscape each week? *(You will need to spend double this time for the first two years to establish the garden. If more than one person will be doing maintenance give a break down for each person per week.)*

4) Total you are comfortable investing in the installation of your landscape over time $

5) If doing this work in stages how do you see it breaking down:

- Now:$
- Year Two:$
- Year Three: $
- Yearly thereafter: $

6) [[[Note about stages: *Anything can be broken into stages, based either on the sequence that will be the most efficient to install (this saves you money) or the order of priority that is most important for you.* See chapters on doing gardens in stages and "How to Save Money" to learn more.

7) Are you interested in doing any aspects of the installation yourself?

- Design?
- Demolition of existing landscape?
- Hardscape installation?
- Putting in a waterfall?
- Amending soil?
- Planting plants?
- Adding drip irrigation?
- Adding low-voltage lighting?
- Spreading bark?
- Clean up?

8) Are there specific dates for beginning/completion you wish to work around?

Suggestion: You may wish to walk around the entire garden and take notes of anything you like, don't like, observe that needs repair etc.

Note: If you don't know the answers to any of these questions or can't make up your mind don't worry. You have two ways of getting to know yourself better. One is to do additional research to get to know your tastes. You can do this by pausing next time you see a garden you really like or dislike and using the questionnaire to break it down. Is it the colors you don't like or just the scale? Is it the shapes or the textures? Which plants do you like and why? By making your response to a garden conscious and detailed you are educating yourself about what you do and do not like in a way that will be necessary to confidently create a design you will enjoy. It is particularly important to understand when working with professionals that if you don't know what you want, they CERTAINLY don't know what you want, which makes any money you spend from that place of uncertainty a risky bet.

Making Good Landscape Decisions

There are three things you need to know before you can make good landscape decisions.

1. What you value in order of priority (you have already done this two chapters ago).

2. What your options are (you can develop this further with a combination of looking through landscape books, Google searches, consulting with designers and brainstorming).

3. How each of your options affects your values (all the chapters in the previous section of the book provide information on this).

A good landscape decision is one that furthers ALL your four core values AND as many of your other values as possible with the least amount of cost. Let's assume that your ideal definition of success, taking it to a more personal level, is as follows:

1. Improve the net value of my home after expenses/ 10.

2. Spend the least amount of money up-front doing it and not more than $25,000.00/ 10.

3. Have the landscape feel complete within three years/ 7.

4. Keep maintenance costs under $300.00/month/ 10.

5. Include a basketball hoop/ 7.

6. Have ornamental grasses and large stone boulders in the beds by the driveway/ 6.

7. Add an extra parking place/ 5.

8. Include red and orange flowers /9.

9. Include fragrance/ 7.

10. Attract hummingbirds/ 3.

In this example numbers 1,2,4,8 would be your core values. The other things on your list are important to pursue ONLY when doing so is not in significant conflict with these four.

Let's look at two different design options using your numbers in a mathematical formula to measure how good the ideas are, relative to your values:

The first scenario is leveling a portion of the garden and creating a separate area for a basketball hoop and play area on brushed concrete

- Your low bid for the work is $15,000.00, more than half of your total budget.
- After talking with your realtor, she does not think it will appeal to the typical buyer and may detract from property value.
- It would be almost no maintenance, once built.
- It does not contribute to any of your other values.

Here is how we measure this idea:

- Let's give it a zero for improving the value of your home.
- Let's give it a zero for helping the budget.
- Since this would feel complete instantly it gets a 7
- Since it lowers maintenance we'll give it a 10'
- It adds a basketball hoop so we'll give the idea 7 points for that line-item.
- We'll give it a zero for all other line-items.

Total points in favor of the idea: 24 points.

Total CORE value points in favor of the idea: 10, for reducing maintenance.

In the second scenario you develop an idea that synergistically furthers several of your core values simultaneously. By analyzing your design you realize that if your current parking area near the house is expanded just four feet you can park an additional car. In order to mask the difference between the old and new concrete you will decoratively stain the entire parking area so that it has a natural rock look and can double as a patio. The bigger area also is now wide enough to add a portable basketball hoop on one side. And because no major grading needs to be done this entire idea can be done for $12,000.00.

Here's how we measure this idea:

- Your real-estate agent thinks that the foux-stone finish and extra parking place will increase curb appeal and add $15,000.00 in property value, so we'll give this a 9.
- By turning a large and ugly part of the existing landscape (the parking area) into something more decorative there is less pressure to up-grade the surrounding landscape and it's cheaper than any other idea being reviewed so we'll give it seven points 7 for budget.
- It instantly makes the landscape feel more complete so we'll give it all 7 points for that.
- It eliminates regular maintenance for the new parking area but because less square footage will be poured in concrete. We will give it a 6 in the maintenance category.
- It does not take up as much room as the stand-alone court so there is more room for ornamental grasses and boulders so we'll give it a 3 for that line item.
- It adds the parking place so gets 5 points for that.
- It does not take up as much room, allowing more room for orange and red flowers so it gets 5 points there.
- We'll give it 5 more points for the last two values:

Total points in favor of the idea: 47

Total core value points in favor of the idea: 26

In other words the second idea is more than TWICE as valuable to you as the first one and is cheaper. And this is simply between these two ideas. There is undoubtedly a third option that is even better. This is the power and value of imaginative synergistic thinking in alignment with your clearly defined values. When this pattern of good or bad decisions is extrapolated over an ENTIRE landscape it explains why many poorly designed landscapes are actually more expensive than well-designed landscapes that bring more value to their owner.

Do you see how this works? It is a process of COMPARING how each choice you make affects each of the things that are important to you. And it works on every level of a garden. If you are choosing between two plants you must first define what you are looking for in a plant in both practical AND aesthetic terms.

I'm looking for a plant that:

- Costs less than $10.00 per plant
- Is deer resistant.
- Is evergreen.
- Has year round interest.
- Has a "cottage garden" look.
- Does well in full sun.
- Is cold-hardy for this area.
- Is not poisonous.
- Grows 2-4 high.
- Does not require any chemicals to keep it healthy.
- Has pink flowers.

Daphne Odora may come to mind. How does it compare to all the other plants that meet these criteria in your eyes? Whether you do the math on every decision or not, it's important to understand the concept and use it to create excellent decisions!

Creating a Scaled As-Built

An "as-built" is an accurate rendition on paper of what is currently built. This is achieved by drawing everything on a reduced scale. 1/8"= 1' is a common scale because it is about 100 times smaller than the actual site and will likely fit onto a sheet of drafting paper.

Do you NEED an as-built? This partially depends on you and what will come next. Benefits of an as-built include:

- After you create one and make copies you can create numerous sketches that have an accurate relationship with your site. You can ultimately use your as-built to record your final design.

- If you want to get multiple bids from contractors you will need to present clear drawings showing the house, existing landscape and the new design to scale. An as-built is step one of a scaled design.

- If you want to take a clear drawing to such places as the Urban Farmer for free irrigation design help you will need to give them an accurate drawing of your new landscape.

- If you visualize best on paper you will want to begin with formal drawings.

- If your landscape is intended to be particularly formal (i.e. the lines of the house extend perfectly out into the landscape) you will have a better overview doing this on paper first.

Situations where you may want to save the trouble of creating either an as-built OR formal drawings include:

- You are doing the work yourself and are good at visualizing on the ground.

- *Your design is simple and you are spray-painting it on the ground (you can always take measurements of your spray-painted areas separately for the purpose of calculating the quantity of materials needed – which is a lot easier than a scaled as-built of an ENTIRE site in accurate relationship to house and itself).*

- *You prefer to use colored flags on the ground to create a plant-count rather than drawing all the plants out.*

There are several ways to obtain a scaled as-built:

- It may already exist as a site plan associated with the architectural drawings for the house. If you can't find this go the Civic Center and check in the building department to see what plans they have on file. If you find it, do some measurements on site to make sure that this is accurate. If it is, you are in luck.

- Hire a surveyor or landscape designer to help you create your as-built from scratch. They will do this by first locating the property corners and then taking measurements between the property corners and each fixed land-mark on the site using long tape measures.

- Use a computer program to digitally do the process I'm going to describe manually below.

- Create one yourself. To prepare yourself gather:

  o Go to youtube and look up hand-drafting and scaled drawings if you are unfamiliar with geometry and have never drafted anything so you can get some pictures in your mind of what I'm describing.

  o A 300' tape measure

  o A right-angle drafting ruler

o A piece of stiff backing with a large sheet of gridded drafting paper attached

o A scaled ruler with the scale you want to use

o A pencil and eraser

o A drafting compass that can open big enough to encompass (pun intended) your biggest measurement in the scale you have chosen (i.e. if your biggest measurement is 230' and you pick 1/8" = 1' scale you will want to have a compass that can open to 29".

o You will also want to make sure you know where at least two of your property corners are. You can now proceed to create the drawing:

o Using your scaled ruler and the property plot plan (this will come with your real estate documents), create an accurate drawing in your chosen scale of the property on your sketch pad. Since drafting paper is also tracing paper the easiest approach, if you can find a plot plan in your scale, is to tape the plot plan.

o Make a few copies of your plot plan

o Use one of these copies to create a rough sketch of all of the fixed items on your property, such as your house (with all corners roughly sketched), your garage, every major tree, driveway etc.

o Ask an assistant to help you

Now you are ready to begin recording each of the fixed landmarks on your property on your plot plan:

o Using your tape measure, the distance between property corner "a" and two separate corners of your house and write these measurements down on your rough sketch.

- o Now do the same thing from property corner "b." These four measurements are enough information to accurately pinpoint the house on the property.

- o Repeat this process for every building and fixed item on the property.

- o Now measure every face/edge of each building, including decks and patios. As you do, write these on your sketch so that you know what each measurement is for. You are now done with your assistant, who has been holding the tape measure at each one of your fixed points.

- o You can now go to a comfortable table inside to translate your rough sketch and measurements into an accurate as-built.

- o Using another of your accurate site-plans taped onto your board, recreate your measuring sequence on this plot plan. To do this, set your drafting compass to the measurements you have written down, using your scale ruler. If corner "a" on your house was 42' from the north west house corner, set your compass to 42 eighths of an inch and go to about where you think that house corner is on your drawing and make a two inch arc there. Now go to property corner "b" and repeat the process. Where your two arcs intersect is the location of that house corner.

- o Now do the same for the second house corner. At this point you can use your right-angle ruler and your scale ruler to draw out the rest of the house, using the measurements you have taken from each house face. Follow the house around and you should be within 2' of accuracy when the two sides of the house meet up on your drawing.

- o Do this same process for every other fixed aspect of your landscape. With trees you just triangulate to one point on the trunk and draw the trunk to scale using your scale ruler.

- o Curves are harder to calculate so more measurements need to be taken. Curves usually require that at least three points are measured, along with how far away from one another those points are.

Does this seem like a lot of work? It is and its hardly the most exciting part of design. It can take more time to create a good as-built than it takes to create a good design on that as-built. Surveyors often charge thousands of dollars to create an accurate as-built using specialized equipment that is several feet more accurate than you are likely to be with your tape measure. It's one of the reasons that I'm happy when most of my design clients choose a design approach that relies less on scaled drawings and more on a mix of notes, supporting photographs, spray-chalked lines and mini flags to show on the site itself how everything fits together.

On the positive side, this time-consuming process greatly increases your intimate knowledge of your property and can support you in stepping outside of your feelings of familiarity just a bit. This is always helpful when imagining something entirely different than you have grown accustomed to.

Design Principles

Design principles are values but they are bigger than the values and priorities we choose for any one project and function in parallel to everything you have already learned and clarified. These are the values we use to guide ALL design decisions on ALL projects, regardless of the budget, environment, practical needs or preferences of those involved and in that may be considered our chosen design philosophy.

For example, the first principle I design with is "minimum effort for maximum result." This comes from the value I and most of my clients share of getting the most value for the time, energy and money we spend, REGARDLESS of what we are doing. If I am installing a landscape and there is a $10.00 dollar tool that will do the same job as a $50.00 tool I will buy the $10.00 tool. If my clients can hire a landscaper to create the same garden for half the price as another landscaper, all things being equal, they will pick the lower-cost company. Why? Because the money saved can be used to buy other things they value. The same is true of energy: All things being equal if there is a shorter way to get to work, we will take that route and save time and gas so that we can spend that energy doing something more productive than sitting in traffic.

Almost everyone will relate to this value, but it is still subjective. The important thing is to be clear on what our design principles are. Below are the principles that I use, along with some brief examples of how I apply them in the design process. I've chosen this particular set of values because they provide a clear path to get from chaos to a finished garden that most of my clients are extremely happy with. You can borrow all or parts of it or develop your own design philosophy.

Minimum effort for maximum result:

"Result" has everything to do with what you value. That's why it is great that you have already clarified how you define success. If you value low maintenance, beauty, safety and a place to play soccer, then "minimum effort for maximum result" means the quickest, easiest way to achieve this goal to your satisfaction with the least amount of money.

This is fairly straight forward and applies to the overall design. However, it also applies to every small decision within the design. Let's say there are two types of stone you are considering as the material for your retaining wall. One of them is a square Three-River's stone for $640.00 per ton and the other is Sonoma Fieldstone for $140.00 per ton. Now let's say that you like the Three-River's stone 30% more than you like the Sonoma Fieldstone. You like the purple and the square look more than you like the round look, but the Sonoma Fieldstone is also a good choice in your eyes.

Applying the principle of "minimum effort for maximum result" analyzes the added value in RELATIONSHIP to the added cost. You would not pay $45.00 dollars for a $10.00 bottle of shampoo just because it had 30% more shampoo than the typical $10.00 bottle of shampoo. In the same way, it does not make sense to spend 400% more money for a stone choice that you only like 30% more than the cheaper alternative. Saving $500.00 per ton on a four- ton wall will allow you to spend that $2,000.00 in some other area of the landscape that will hopefully give you $8,000.00 in value – an instant 400% return on investment!

Of course it is not just the cost to "like" ratio. To apply this principle well includes ALL of your values, which is why it's helpful to be clear on what they are and their order of priority for you. Things to consider include:

- What is the cost?
- What is the quality?
- How much you like it?

- How easy is it to maintain?
- How long it will last before needing to be replaced?
- Will it add property value?
- Will it complement what's around it the most?
- Is it safe for children?
- How easy is it to install/buy?

There are some things that even if they are "free" are too expensive in other areas to be worth the overall cost (try having a friend give you boat when you don't really want one or use it enough to justify all the money to maintain it and the space to store it). Other things are cheap even costing twice as much money initially because they accomplish so MANY of your other values simultaneously.

It is very helpful if the person designing a landscape looks through these eyes. Doing so naturally results in increased creativity, sustainability and value at ALL levels of the project, not just material selection.

Form follows function:

This principle begins with valuing comfortable living. If you want to pick fresh herbs and vegetables this principle dictates that they will be placed close to the kitchen so that they can be harvested without a hassle when you remember them at the last minute while cooking. It dictates that pathways be placed where it is most comfortable and practical to walk, not worked in as a last-minute thought after designing interesting flower arrangements.

Applying this principle leads to such things as driving your car around in the dirt and turning around BEFORE the driveway is poured in concrete and you are left feeling cramped every day for the next ten years when you try and turn around. In short, the shape of any object or feature in a landscape is dictated by the living habits and preferences of the individual home-owner and not the other way around.

Another important application of this principle is to start by designing to achieve the three to five really important functions or goals of a project and then let the smaller items fit into the cracks or not. If your priority is not spending a penny over $30,000.00, getting a very safe no-maintenance driveway to park three cars and having a patio with a bench, the place to start is not going online to look at bench prices. The place to start is to research and design a really great driveway. And for that matter, since for many of us our driveways are almost as big as the front gardens, it does not necessarily make sense to go for the cheapest no-maintenance driveway if it is also the ugliest. In fact, doing a stamped concrete driveway that costs $28,000.00 and spreading wild-flowers on the bare soil and keeping an eye out on Craig's list for a free bench and some patio stone may be the way to go. Far better than having a Smith and Hawken bench and a designer patio, only to realize that there is no money for anything but an ugly driveway from a low-balling contractor who does not take the time to form up a shape that makes it easy to turn around or have pleasing lines that complement the house. Begin by doing the big things well and let the others fall through the cracks.

Relationship:

This principle reminds us that a landscape does not exist in isolation. The front yard is in relationship to the back yard. The entire yard is in relationship to the neighborhood and surrounding areas. The landscape is in relationship to the house and all of it is in relationship with you, the home-owner.

The principle of relationship reflects the value of consistency and integration between the big picture as well as the details. It should be obvious to the casual observer on an instinctive level that the person designing the back garden was aware of the existence of the front garden, the neighborhood and the house.

There are a number of ways to accomplish this goal. One of them is with the use of shapes and lines. For example, starting a bed at the exact corner of a house shows awareness of the house. Doing the bed in a scale that is appropriate for the size of the house also shows awareness for the house. Creating shapes within the garden that complement or echo other shapes in the garden shows that one area of the garden was done with awareness of the other areas.

Psychologically, this makes us feel more peaceful and relaxed. Just as we tend to tense up when an individual is behaving in a way that is inappropriate and awkward in a group, to a lesser degree we tense up when we see a shape, color or object that seems to clash with everything else in the garden.

Balance of attention:

We feel most peaceful when our attention is centered and balanced. Here are some of the forces that affect our sense of balance and direct our attention:

- **Grading**: Like water, our attention naturally runs downhill. If we are perched on the top of a hill our eyes will naturally come to rest at the bottom.
- **Light**: Our eyes and attention will always move towards the light and will stay there, providing it is not blinding.
- **Lines**: Our eyes will follow a line and come to rest at the end of it.
- **Height**: The higher and steeper a solid mass is (such as a sheer wall on a three story house), the more our body instinctively wants to move away from it, both visually and physically, to get more perspective.
- **Sound:** Our attention is drawn in the direction of sound and stays there, providing the sound is not unpleasant.

- **Movement**: Our eyes are drawn to anomalies in a pattern (color, shape or texture) and movement relative to stillness. By introducing an anomaly we can draw attention in that direction. If the movement is pleasant, such as water flowing in a brook, it will tend to hold our gaze.
- **Discomfort:** Our attention is drawn to discomfort to analyze it for possible threats or to do something about it.

A designer creates an overall sense of balance by creating many individual imbalances, much like a child's mobile is counter balanced by many weights and crossbars. Perhaps the grade takes the eye away by falling down hill, but a massive tree is used to interrupt the attention on its way down the hill and bring us back to ourselves. A gap in the trees draws the eye with brighter light to the left, while the placement of a fountain to the right draws our attention in that direction. Overall, there is a sense of balance, that can be either very still or very dynamic, depending on how intensely we use the forces that direct our attention in juxtaposition with one another. Stepping outside the context of landscapes for a moment, Cirque Du Soleil uses these dynamic imbalances to pull our attention first to one part of the stage then to another, but always holds our attention on the stage. The goal applying this principle to your garden is to have your attention come to rest in key stationary areas, such as a bench, a patio or the front porch.

Scale:

Scale is a distinct sub-category of the principle of relationship. In order for our eye to experience the relationship between objects, scale is essential. Typically if one object is more than five times bigger or smaller than the object next to it, particularly if it is a different color, texture or shape, we start to see them as two unrelated objects rather than a composition of things in relationship to one another.

Imagine a three story flat wall that is all one texture and color. When looking towards this wall our sense of scale will typically be determined by it, as the biggest object. Let's say it is thirty five feet tall and forty feet wide. Using our principle of not going five times bigger or smaller, we might design a bed at the base of this wall that is forty feet long and between eight and twenty feet wide in different sections. In order to strengthen the relationship with the house we might begin and end it at a house corner. Then inside the bed we might plant one fifteen foot wide by thirty foot tall tree, thus breaking up the uninterrupted mass of the house. And below we might put groups of plants in masses ten feet long by three to fifteen feet wide. In this way the bed is in scale with the house. The tree is in scale with the house and the bed. And the lower plantings are in scale with the tree and the bed.

Of course, everything is ultimately in relationship with our own bodies. We would tend to feel out of place when standing next to one of the great pyramids alone in the desert because the awesome scale of our surroundings relative to our own five to six foot tall body highlights how small we are. The pyramid may fit in the desert, but we don't seem to fit well with either, unless we have a car nearby and can focus on that as our scale comparison.

Scale also relates to distance. The farther we are away from something the smaller it appears, relative to our own body and the things around us. What this means is that in addition to being aware of the scale of objects to one another, we need to consider the distance from which they will be viewed. For example, the delicate shape of blue-bell flowers will be perfectly clear when planted on a pot on the deck, but viewed from one hundred feet away you might need to plant fifty times more bluebells in order for the color blue to be briefly noticed by the casual observer.

In summary: the greater the distance, the bigger the scale needs to be to have a similar result. This can be a bit counter-intuitive because when we are PLANTING a bed we are only three feet away from the plants we plant. It will be natural to think: "This feels a bit boring – let me liven things up," when we are planting fifty of the same small plants and stand back a few feet away. The important thing to remember is that while it may look boring from three to five feet away, it will look perfectly in scale and a pleasing splash of interest when viewed from one hundred feet away.

In areas that will be viewed from two distinct distances, perhaps five feet and one hundred feet, as might be the case when a path leads us by a bed that is mainly viewed at a distance from the deck, it's good to have two themes. The main planting can be a unified theme of color, texture or shape, while a border theme that is much smaller can provide contrast, scale and interest for the person walking by.

Another thing that impacts our choice of scale is the speed at which an object is viewed. You may have noticed how very simple highway landscaping is. That is because at fifty five miles an hour it takes literally HUNDREDS of one type of shrub when viewed from thirty feet away for it to have the kind of impact on your eye that just ONE shrub will have when you are standing still three feet away. Understanding this, highway planners do not plant on a typical scale of three to ten feet, but use a scale of fifty to hundreds of feet and keep the plantings simple. This provides the most restful experience for the eye when we drive by at high speeds. It also helps to minimize the enormous scale of our highways and overpasses by juxtaposition.

Balance between boredom and chaos, formality and informality:

The most popular gardens in history achieve this kind of balance in different ways. Some of the most modern and angular homes are landscaped with completely native plants to look like nature. Many of the most symmetrical and formal hardscapes are graced with an abundance of overflowing plants that soften the lines. When just one of these extremes is present the garden feels either rigid or disturbing. Both elements are important. The more one extreme is present, the more the opposite extreme is important to bring in to create an overall balance.

Some common ways to apply this principle include:

- A very well-organized hardscape that is planted with either very simple and natural plantings or a profusion of chaotic plantings. In other words, a formal hardscape with an informal planting.
- Very colorful plantings planted in a very organized pattern.
- Using all one type of tree in a symmetrical pattern (such as forming an arch along a driveway) with a profusion of mixed wildflowers as the ground-cover.
- Using just a few varieties of plants (simple) but arranging them in asymmetrical and varied shapes (complex).
- Using common textures (such as pathway materials and mulches) for both front and back gardens, but varying the plantings so that each area looks both unique and integrated with the whole garden.
- Defining the shapes of beds, paths etc. to echo the lines and shapes of the house in scale, while introducing extremely loud and dramatic art that does not appear to have any direct connection with the environment.

Choosing a Style:

This principle, along, with the following principle on themes, is both a principle and a tool for organizing all the other principles in this chapter. A style is an overall pattern of aesthetic values that help to bring unity to the entire landscape. It is helpful as a designer to begin a project by articulating a style because this will set a tone that can intuitively guide all of your decisions.

Here's how it can help you. Let's say that you want the garden to feel deeply relaxing, subtle and minimalistic. That can sound vague and leaves you to determine "is this stone or plant more or less minimalistic than this other one?" It's sometimes hard to say when these questions are approached without first picking a style. Imagine now that as you described the feeling of your landscape, a Japanese garden had come to mind. Picking this as your style, it immediately helps you to integrate and organize your smaller decisions. Now you have a concept in your mind and as you peruse plants, visit rock suppliers and consider a water-feature you can ask yourself: Is this something I can imagine in a serene, minimalistic Japanese garden?

You can even get a few picture books on Japanese gardens, pick your favorite pictures and then analyze what creates the look you like best:

- How many plant varieties per 100 square feet of garden are there?
- What are the colors used?
- What type of stone is used and how big are the stones relative to the area?
- What is the scale used to define the patterns?
- What shapes are present in the picture and which materials define them?
- What are the plant varieties used and would they grow well in my garden conditions?

Choosing a style not only makes it easier to organize and integrate any number of smaller decisions, it helps the observer experience the garden as a whole when you are done. If it is a well-known style, such as a Japanese Garden, everyone will recognize it. But even if you consciously invent your own style and then stick to it, your garden will still feel unified.

What is a style? It is a template or set of guidelines that result in a recognizable feeling and look, regardless of where and how it is applied. For example, you will recognize the Japanese style on a rooftop garden in Tokyo or a San Francisco park if the garden includes such things as Japanese maples, bonsai, light colored small gravel raked in a pattern, black pines and granite stones with perhaps a stone sculpture of a Japanese tea house.

To build your own style, begin with the feeling you want to have:

- How playful or somber?
- How new or old?
- How loud or quiet, subtle or bold?
- How cool/hip or traditional?

When you have captured the feeling you want in words that make sense to YOU, you can start to develop themes that support your style.

Themes:

Whereas a style is a theme for the entire garden, a theme is a style for a particular area or element within the garden. Going back to the Japanese garden, here are a few of the themes that are common:

- A color scheme of red, green, white and black.
- A scale/shape theme that echoes a natural environment on a smaller scale, using mostly curves and asymmetrical patterns.
- A minimalistic theme that typically limits plant varieties to seven plants or less.
- A material theme that consists of gravel, stone, bamboo and sometimes black wrought iron.

As you develop themes for your own custom style, it might look something like this:

- Asymmetrically curving walls in a snake shape 2-4' high using cinder block and broken stain glass mosaic as the surface with glass in neon colors with white grout.
- All screening done with different types of bamboo ranging from 6'-30' contained in stainless steel circles 3-4' wide that are buried 12" and rise 18" from the ground.
- 1" Mexican pebbles as the mulch between plantings.
- 2-3' high dwarf Rhododendrons as the understory anywhere there is bamboo.
- All other plants to be a mix of ornamental grasses and succulents, mostly, with a predominance of blue and then brown foliage. Planting scale to range between five and fifteen feet.
- Lighting to be done with a mix of fiber optic spots woven into bamboo perimeter, copper pathway lights with a modern angular look, and flood lights with changing color gels using pink, purple, blue and clear.
- Water-feature to be raised, circular and have evenly balanced fountain jets with a lining of Mexican pebbles and fiber optic lights at the bottom.

Once themes are developed that support the feeling you want to have, following these themes will create a certain look whether it is a six hundred square foot garden or a twenty thousand square foot garden. The particular themes I've made up on the spot for this example, create a mix of natural beauty and aliveness. It might be appropriate for a Disney garden, certain hotels, a modern mansion or a business focusing on creativity, vitality and seeking to attract employees or clients who like a hip/modern look.

In the case of your themes, you want to make sure that they are the easiest way to create the kind of feeling you have defined as your style. You can do this by making up a bunch of different themes, examining costs, maintenance implications etc. of each one and then picking those that bring you the most value for the cost. In the bonus section at the end of the book I've included a mini-encyclopedia I created for myself to remind me of many styles, themes and other patterns available to include in a landscape.

As we conclude this chapter on the design principles I've chosen as the basis for my design decisions, do they make sense to you? They are not the only principles you can choose and not even necessarily the best principles. They are simply a set of tools that I've developed that bring me a consistent experience of pleasing success. You can pick whatever principles you wish to guide your decisions. For them to be useful, however, when making the hundreds of decisions you will need to make, you will need to clearly define them so that you can use them as a conscious reference point when you are facing a choice.

Using Google Images and Books

If you have not used Google to search images you are in for a treat. It's not perfect but it can be a powerful tool to help you visualize ideas and expand your thinking outside the box. When I teach classes and a student asks to see examples of something I'm talking about it is easy to do a quick search on Google on such topics as "whimsical fences" and then click the "images" tab so that only photographs related to the search will show. In the case of whimsical fences, it will show you more than one hundred photos, many of which may spark an idea or expand your sense of what can be done.

Seeing pictures of what other people around the world have done relating to your topic is a huge step in the direction of expanding your mind beyond the ideas you may currently be considering. If just one change occurs as a result that saves you money, time or results in a look that brings you joy, it has been well worth your while.

Google images, books and outside input can be an antidote to what I consider the biggest and most invisible problem for novice landscapers: Namely not knowing enough to realize that for the same amount of time and money something much more in sync with your values could have been created that you are not bothered by because in your imagination it does not exist. When we don't know what we can do, we are often quite happy with what we are planning to do. However, when we introduce more possibilities we may quickly realize that what we thought was a great idea is an OK idea. There are in fact a number of better ways to do things, some costing less money to install and less time to maintain.

Preparing for your design with images:

Gather at least three images that you like for each aspect you are considering for you design. If you want to have a seating area with a bench, gather at least three photos of a bench and seating areas. At this stage you can also research some of the costs of things like benches – particularly if you gather your pictures from online catalogs or at local nurseries.

Creating Your Design

Everything up until this point has been designed to bring your mind to the point where you can intelligently choose between the infinite options available to you in a way that is most consistent with your values. It's helpful to have a way of parallel thinking as you examine your ideas and to intuitively shift your emphasis between your values as you go along. You may notice that one idea absolutely DELIGHTS you so it makes sense to shift focus to the fact that ultimately that is what ALL of this is about. In another moment you may draw a blank and rely entirely on an analysis of the facts that you synthesize from this book and perhaps some additional research. In another moment you may notice that your partner is PASSIONATE or ADAMANT about some particular detail. If that's the case it probably makes more sense for the benefit of your relationship to pay more attention to their feelings in that area than to whether or not their request strengthens or weakens your themes. If you have a toddler that might get hurt it makes sense to do the things at WHATEVER cost that will keep them safe. There are many things that are important and many good ways to go about them. As long as you are staying in sync with your strongest overall values and are confident you are not spending a lot of money to create a mess you are going to be fine. Because there are so many variables to juggle, when you are all done, it is wise to bring in a professional or some good friends with landscape experience to review your choices to make sure you are not making any glaring mistakes!

At this stage you have most of the practical information you need and you have your to-scale drawing of the house and property. As importantly, you have your written answers to the landscape questionnaire and you have a clear definition of what you would call success. Congratulations! You have prepared more thoroughly than 95% of all people, with or without professional help, who begin a landscape design! And if you decide to take a few short-cuts or skip some of the steps I suggest, don't feel bad. Everything that you apply will help you and using any of it is a LOT better than nothing. If spending only $20.00 and reading this book improves your thought-process even 10% you are profiting handsomely from your investment. However, if you have very little money to create your landscape, remember that every mistake avoided on paper costs ten times less than a mistake made in the field. If you really work with this book and do your homework extensively there is a good chance you will avoid ALL mistakes and make your money go a long way.

There is a lot of landscape and design knowledge that is factual and fairly linear. It is easy to package it into little boxes of accurate information that will be useful. This is harder to do with the CREATIVE process that uses all of this information in a unique way to create a garden that only YOU would create. So for this, the most important section of the book, I've taken a different approach. Rather than telling you what you SHOULD do, I'm going to share with you my unique way of working with this material and some of my thought processes behind it. It is intended as a template for you to follow UNLESS you feel moved to go about it differently in a way that works better for you. All that is important is that the end result expresses your personal values and priorities.

When clients hire me to create a design it is at about this stage in the book that I walk on to the project. I have looked at their questionnaire, talked with them about their value hierarchies, looked at any pictures they have gathered and possibly walked around the garden with them for twenty minutes listening to some of their ideas and complaints. Often the as-built has been provided to me by making a copy of the site-plan.

I design best while walking around the site. I'll often start out on the road and walk up the road until the house/garden begins to come into view. I'll notice how it affects me. Does it invite me in? Is it clear where to go? Does the scale seem right? What hits me? I continue to walk up the driveway and to the front door, all the while noticing the impressions I have. And I don't confine it to landscaping. My observations might be something like this:

- Mailbox is the first thing you see and it's falling over with peeling paint.
- House seems intimidating – too big for the lot and is perched on a hill.
- Huge driveway is cracked.
- Big wall on left side of the house is bare – needs a tree or something to make it less imposing.
- Front door is invisible from driveway – hard to see where to go.
- House-colors seem jarring.
- Carport dominates the view.

If a person has indicated a desire to profitably sell their home these things will all have bearing. If a person likes to entertain these things will also have bearing. I notice which of my impressions seem most relevant to the client's priorities and which of the many options for addressing them will fit within the client's stated budget. I encourage you to begin with a similar overall analysis.

Once you have done the initial approach and walk to the front door, continue to take notes of your impressions from all key windows and from key vantage points as you walk along the paths. If it helps, you can bring a video camera and record your comments to watch later.

When you are done, rate your observations on a 1-10 scale to help you focus in on what's important. Perhaps you notice a power pole from several key windows and locations and you give that a 10 to indicate that blocking that in some way is a very high priority. Start brainstorming different ways of solving the problem. With a power pole you might think of things such as planting several tall narrow junipers or cypresses that block the pole from each of the angles it is viewed from. If you are going to put in a shed, consider making it taller and analyze the pros and cons of placing it in a position that blocks the view of the pole. In some situations it may be worth exploring your options for removing one or more power-poles and placing the related wires underground. I have seen these costs typically range from between $10-50,000.00 and involve a fair amount of paperwork and sometimes neighbor cooperation.

Do this analysis with each of your high priority items. Practice thinking outside the box. When you are all done weigh the pros and cons to each approach. You are then in a position to assess which of your ideas have the most merit when filtered through such things as the answers to your questionnaire, your definition of success, your style and other design principles.

This is the really fun part of design. It is as if you have a large array of vegetables and a cutting board in front of you and you get to decide which vegetables to cook with today, how thickly to slice them, whether to fry, bake or steam them and how to spice them up a bit. Every choice you make will affect the health and flavor of the meal you ultimately sit down to eat. You can be sure that there has never been a garden quite like yours. Can you come up with a plan that you will enjoy living in and that reflects your values?

Once I have identified the key problems, the key potentials for improvement and what will probably need to change for the landscape to become more in alignment with my client's values, I start imagining the new design. I start with the functional and the large things. If the driveway needs to be expanded/contracted I look at that. If shade needs to be added I assess where the big trees need to be. If there will be a water-feature I analyze the place that will be the most impactful. Imagining living in the home, I notice where my body feels most comfortable walking from one location to another. And once I am confident in an idea, I get out my water based striping paint and I spray down lines. If it's a path, I mark both edges of the path with paint and then walk within the lines to see how my body feels about walking in that location. If I'm feeling overshadowed by a tall building I might move the path away a bit. If I feel like I'm walking into a big tree I might go around it or decide to prune some of the lower branches of the tree.

At this stage of the design it is all about shapes, elevations and lines. I'm not worrying about whether the expanded driveway will be pavers, stamped concrete or brick. I'm focusing on things such as: is there enough room for all the cars to be parked AND turn around? What will this shape look like when viewed from the upstairs living room window? Are the curves comfortable for a typical car to make? First come the lines and only after everything fits together will I worry about colors, textures and materials.

Once I have the rough outline of the entire landscape in place on a functional level, with all walls, paths, water-features, driveways, arches, gazebos and anything else that is structural clearly marked out with paint, I assign ball-park costs to everything and assess how we are doing in relationship to the budget. After years of bidding things, I generally know before I even paint things out about what things will cost but you will probably need to take measurements, calculate costs of different types of materials and then determine whether or not your design requires any modifications. If, for example, you discover that using even the cheapest materials you can only do half of what you want to do, you may need to make some hard choices:

- Do I go for what I want and do the project in stages?
- Do I scale back my ideas a lot and use top-notch materials?
- Do I do the work myself?
- Do I scale back my ideas a little and use lower end materials?
- Do I use top-notch materials in half the areas that really matter to me and use low-cost materials in the rest?
- Do I raise the budget?

I personally do not think a garden is worth stressing too much about. After all, if you did absolutely nothing you would have mostly native something growing on most of your bare dirt in a matter of years and that is not such a tragedy, regardless of what the neighbors think. If you have determined a budget that you are comfortable spending, I generally think it is good to stick to that budget rather than stressing out, unless you are going to stress out even more about not getting something you have your heart set on. I also think it's best to build your relationship with your family rather than your garden. If someone in your family is anxious around money you will all probably be happier if you respect those feeling rather than push past them to get a more luxurious garden. Our relationships typically affect how we feel in the long run more than any garden will.

I don't proceed past this stage of rough design until I am confident that there is enough money in the budget to install the design. This saves a LOT of time and is one of the reasons that 90% of my initial ideas get installed fairly close to their original concept. To avoid being in the camp of the many who feel stressed, drained and broke after a big project that was not properly managed, I invite you to do the same.

Once I have the "bones" of the landscape designed, I start working on planting themes and specific hardscape materials. This is when I take a client to the rock-yard to examine all the different types of wall-stone, flag-stone, boulders and gravel. This is also when we start zeroing in on fence-details etc. I personally find it helpful to establish a practical budget BEFORE going out to look at materials and focusing the client's attention on the materials that work within that budget. However, if they are interested, they can always ask about the cost of other materials and they have the freedom to increase the budget if they fall in love with anything that is more expensive. This focus on a pre-established budget discourages frivolous expenses but still leaves room for change in areas a client feels strongly about.

When I set up budgets for items before going out shopping, I do so based on the functional and passion-value the client expresses for that area. If the fence we are putting up is just for the deer and will be largely screened by some vines growing on it, I'll factor a ball-park budget based on the low-end of materials – unless the client has a large budget and a focus on prestige. For a shed that no one will see, I'll factor a prefabricated low-end shed. But for a large driveway I might allow for top of the line materials because it will make a huge difference on how my client feels about arriving to their home each day, as well as the resale value and appearance of the overall home. Then again, there are a variety of ways of going about that, ranging from giving the client some dyes to play with (if they don't have the money and are open to doing work themselves) to tearing out and pouring a whole new top-of-the-line stamped concrete driveway with built in lighting. Designing is a constant dance between possibilities, values, boundaries and priorities.

The best designs happen when there is no rush. It's hard to come up with an entirely fresh idea when a client is communicating that they would be REALLY happy if we could be done early and don't have to meet again. This is a very easy request to accommodate but may result in a less customized design or a missed opportunity that would have emerged naturally in the conversation if there was space for it. I encourage you to take the time you need with each of these steps, knowing that any idea you have in this stage will typically give you a tenfold return on the time it takes to consider the idea.

I like to pin every cost of every item down in rough numbers before proceeding to refine the idea. If some areas need to be left vague for some reason (say you can't make up your mind and want to make a final decision after part of the garden is built) then figure out the worst-case scenario cost if you made up your mind to pick the most expensive materials

Since you may not have the experience to recognize some of the curve-balls that the site may through at you, if you are designing and installing the landscape yourself, I encourage you to allow 30% extra in your budget for these anomalies. If it does not get used, HOORAY. You will have come in under budget, and become part of the rare 1% anomalies in the construction industry.

To estimate plants at this juncture examine these answers in your questionnaire:

- When do you want your landscape to feel mature?
- How dense or how far apart do you want your plants to be?
- What is your overall budget?

Your answers combine with the following plant costs to give you your budget:

- One gallon plants cost an average of $9.00
- Five gallon plants cost and average of $20.00

- Fifteen gallon plants cost and average of $60.00

If you are hiring someone to plant these plants the labor costs will also go up proportionally because it takes five times more time to dig a five gallon hole than a one gallon hole.

Consider this fact: It typically takes one year for a one gallon plant to become a five gallon plant. It takes typically one-two years for a five gallon plant to become a fifteen gallon plants. Plants are sold by the size of the pot, not the size of the plant so sometimes you will find a bigger pot in a gallon than in a five gallon.

In short, if you can wait three years you can cut your plant costs by around 500% for the same look. If your plants are densely planted every 18" the same plants will cost 50% more than if they are planted 36" apart. By knowing the square footage of the beds you will plant, whether they will be one gallon, five gallon or fifteen gallon plants (specimen trees are more and should be individually researched rather than estimated) and how much spacing there is you can estimate within 15% what your plant budget needs to be BEFORE you even decide what the specific plants will be. This is very helpful when doing an initial budget to make sure that as your design takes shape it is in the ballpark it needs to be to get built. I will typically do some more refining of the plantings and themes after confirming that I can do what I hoped I could do within the client's budget.

At this point it is helpful to draw your spray-painted lines on your site as-built. You may be someone who designs better with spray paint when you can feel the space (like me) or someone who designs better conceptually, in which case you may refine your concepts as you draw them. If you don't relate well to paper at all and you are good at keeping lots of details in your head, it may be enough for you to simply develop your design and install it straight from your spray-painted lines. This is not practical, however, if you want to get accurate competitive bids.

A more organic approach to plant design: When I am designing AND installing a garden I typically like to wait to do the detailed planting plan until AFTER the hardscape is built. Using the formula I just gave you, I develop a planting budget so I can estimate costs, but there is something about looking at the actual bed that is newly built and ready for planting that leads to a more satisfying and accurate design. I also like to save my clients money and it's quite possible that during a month-long project they will come home one day, partially through the project and say "I saw this plant at my sister's – is there anywhere we can put this in?" Now if we had carefully drawn out every plant before beginning the project than this could mean going back to the drawing board to work the plant in. If, on the other hand, we have simply developed basic planting themes, such as "woodland garden, cutting garden with pastel colors, feature tree of some kind 30' tall, and "year round interest entrance plantings 2-5' tall" then it is usually easy to integrate a new plant idea into one of those themes. No time is wasted. When I use this approach I sometimes set out different colored flags to mark where each plant will go and then place the plants I buy next to each flag to make sure I like the look before planting them.

Spontaneity vs. predictability: My general view is that spontaneity and change are fun and easy when they do not interfere with the schedule or blow the budget. When they do, they are something I try and avoid for the benefit of the client. It's more fun to have things done early and on budget than late and over-budget.

Using Photographs to Refine Plant Themes: When refining planting themes it is helpful to start with photographs: "I want bed

"A" to look like this photograph and bed "B" to look like this photograph.

Photos can be a valuable reference point for beginners because you (possibly with the help of nursery staff) can break them down into the recipe of plant varieties, quantities and spacing that created the look you like: "It looks like this bed in the photo is twenty feet by fifteen feet and in that area they are using seven types of plants. As near as I can tell the plants are about four feet apart and there are twenty of them." This information can provide disciple to your instinctual impulse to plant in a way that looks full NOW before all the plants grow (if you succumb to this impulse you will have a mess or have to take out half your plants in a few years).

You can optionally print or photocopy these photos in a scale that lets you cut and glue them into the beds on your design drawing. Another option is taking a picture of your house, printing it out large and then gluing pictures of gardens you like on top of the existing garden in the photo of your house so that you can have a sense of what a photo would look like of your house after you were done landscaping. I sometimes work with a colleague of mine who specializes in using Photoshop to create my design images so realistically that they look like the finished garden!

Ask for help from a nursery: You can work with a knowledgeable nursery to help you technically build up the look you want piece by piece using plants that are appropriate to your particular bed. Plants that touch in the photo may actually be planted three and six feet apart but be 3-5 years older than the one gallon plantings you plan to use. Green Jeans and some of the Sloats staff are quite knowledgeable and helpful. Call around before you go in person and make sure someone knowledgeable is available and has some time on their hands. It is courteous to go during a less time at the nursery and to buy at least some of your plants there to acknowledge the favor they are doing you.

Designing the whole garden: It is important to design the ENTIRE garden at one time before you build any of it. The reason for this is twofold:

- It encourages more thought about how ALL the pieces fit together in ways that can save time and money later.
- Some design possibilities are ONLY feasible in one area if they are integrated in some way with another area. If you do one area first it may be much more expensive to redo it so that it fits with an area you design and install later.

I would estimate that over a twenty year period 40% of long-term home-owners spend 30% or around $15,000 more than they would have spent redoing and modifying and upgrading things than they would have spent creating a much nicer garden carefully from the start and then not changing it. As a designer my goal is to save clients that money AND give them a nicer garden. This is not hard to do because designs cost so little, relative to installation.

Cross referencing specific plants: You have two sets of criteria that each plant needs to meet. The first is your theme, which describes the look:

- Evergreen
- 2-5' tall and narrow
- Pink fragrant flowers
- Variegated big leaves

The second set of criteria is technical.

- Must be deer resistant
- Has to handle heavy clay soil
- Tough enough so my dog wont lay on it
- Non-poisonous for my young child

- Likes partial light

As you make enquiries at local nurseries to find the possibly three to ten available plants that meet ALL these criteria, the final filtering is a combination of the one you like the most AND the one that will work well with your other plantings. You might like one slightly better but it does not go well with the other plants you have chosen. That's one reason to always begin by picking the most impactful plantings first and then pick other plants that compliment them. This will create a more pleasing overall effect than picking plants that you may personally like, but which don't create an overall composition that you like. This principle is similar to a painter using browns and blacks at times to HIGHLIGHT and contrast the bright colors that are the real painting's focus.

Let's review a good checklist to complete before going on to the installation stage. Anything you can say "yes" to gets a check mark:

- I am clear about what I want and what I am willing to spend in time, money and energy to create it.
- I am clear about what will make this project a success for me.
- I have basic technical knowledge relating to all the aspects I have included in my design.
- I am confident that I have budgeted well and the design is within my budget.
- I have a clearly defined style and themes that support it.
- I either have a detailed drawing of plants or a plant budget based on square footage and will develop my final planting plan after the hardscape is built.
- If this is my first landscape project and I'm doing it myself I have reviewed my drawings with a knowledgeable professional or a friend to make sure I am not overlooking

an easier way to do things. I have allowed 30% in my budget for surprises.

A final check-in before making a big commitment: Regardless of whether you have gone through the stages of a good design, there are some important questions to examine at this time. When I am finished with a design for a client I pay attention to the body language of a client:

- Do they seem happy with the design?
- Do they seem confident that this is a wise investment for them?
- Do BOTH people in a couple seem to be on board?

I know that a couple will be happier if they respect one another and do things that both are interested in than they will be with a great garden. I know that there are many ways a client can spend money other than in a new landscape. A design is the CHEAPEST part of the whole project and I consider it quite a good use of a client's money if it helps them clarify that they don't really want to spend the money it will take to get their dreams at this time. The design is equivalent to the relationship stage of being engaged. And it's best to stop now if something does not feel quite right.

The other reason this check-in is important is that there are MANY ways to go about something. Often it just takes a review of the choices and a small revision or clarification to help someone go from feeling OK about the project to feeling great. But the first step is acknowledging that something does not feel quite right with the current plan.

One of the benefits of having a third party present is that sometimes a couple is making unnecessary compromises with one another simply because they lack the knowledge to imagine a third way of doing things that could leave BOTH of them getting all of what they want. When I can provide that I am always happy because again, I know that my client's good relationship will bring them more well-being than I can possibly bring them with a beautiful garden.

Resolving Couple Conflict

I include this chapter in the design section because if you are in a relationship and designing a landscape project together, you will need to negotiate differences well to have a successful project.

Below are approaches I find useful as I help clients find a win/win during the design stage:

- Remember that the relationship is more important than the garden.
- Most things are not an either/or. For example, if one person loves a plant and the other person hates it, move on to another plant. Among 4,500 plants there are probably at least thirty that both of you will like.
- Typically each person will care more about some areas of a garden then others. That's when a 1-10 scale becomes useful. By agreeing to compromise in favor of the person who has the highest number of passion about a given issue ahead of time, typically both people will get what they want in the areas most important to them. This can be put into practice simply by both people giving a number to represent how much they care about this issue. If you are a 10 about doing the more expensive drainage option and your partner is a 5 around preferring the cheaper version, go with the expensive drainage option. Etc. or look for another way to spend money that you are both a strong yes to.
- Agree on a budget you both feel OK with and don't go over it.
- If you both want different things and it feels awkward or dangerous to the relationship to try and sort it out alone, bring in a designer. A good designer may be able to help both of you get what you really want, even though on the

surface you have different ways of going about things. Let's say you want an Asian garden because that feels serene and uncluttered. Your partner wants a cottage English garden that feels cozy and inviting. On the surface you both can't get what you want. But a good designer may be able to show you ways where you feel uncluttered and serene and your partner feels comfortable and invited. It may be a hybrid of the two styles or something entirely different. Often it just takes a new idea to create a breakthrough that leaves everyone feeling happy.

- If one person really cares about the garden and the other does not, it may be simplest to do the whole garden to please the person who really cares about it. The other will benefit more from their partner's happiness in this scenario than by having the garden the way they want it.
- Sometimes personal preference differences can easily be moved beyond when both of you share a higher value, such as resale value. You may have different tastes but if your shared highest value is maximum resale value or lowering your maintenance then both of your preferences can take a back-seat to a design that is not so much about you as it is about the resale market for your type of home.
- Create separate areas within the garden where each of you can get exactly what they want. This makes more sense in a larger garden. In the main garden areas you can create a design that you both like. However in each of your "personal gardens" you can have an agreed area to do WHATEVER you want, whether or not your partner likes it. This can be a place for your favorite plants that your partner hates and vice versa.
- If you are working with a professional designer, it can be helpful to discuss your different values/preferences and how you want to handle them before meeting with a

designer. Otherwise you may feel pressured by the time-constraints of a design-meeting to rush through certain conflicts and damage your relationship in the process.

- If the garden is proving contentious but you are both enthusiastic and clear about going on a vacation, buying a new car etc. then do those things, have fun and perhaps it will put the garden in perspective when you return to it at some point.

These approaches work well for me when working with couples. I hope they work well for you too.

Design Paradigms

For those of you interested in going a little deeper into the design process, it is helpful to be aware of our design paradigms so we can consciously either change or confirm them. Our paradigm is one of the most unconscious and powerful influences in a design process because it affects everything we do but is normally invisible. It is not a direct thought or feeling, but functions as a custom funnel that only allows the thoughts and feelings that fit through our particular funnel to consciously exist.

While a paradigm is not a thought or feeling it is motivated by thoughts and feelings. Some of the common thoughts and feelings we use to create our landscape paradigms include:

- I don't want the neighbors to think I'm inconsiderate or a loser. (Creates the paradigm of: "Landscape for the purpose of looking normal to the neighbors.")
- I want my family to be impressed when they visit. (Creates the paradigm of: "Landscape as a vehicle for proving I am a worthwhile person."
- I don't want anyone to think I'm weird. (Creates the paradigm of "Landscaping as a way to show how normal I am.")
- I want to be looked at like a winner. (Creates the paradigm of "Landscaping to show how successful I am.")
- I want to look and be modern and up to date. (Creates the paradigm of "Landscaping to show that I'm up to date.")
- I want to increase my property value. (Creates the paradigm of "Landscaping to conform to the marketplace.")
- I want to love my partner. (Creates the paradigm of "Landscaping to please my partner.")

All of these paradigms are externally based, which means that the decisions we make go through an interpretive process as we imagine and project what the observer might think: "No... I don't think that would go over well in our neighborhood." Or "Yeah! I saw that look at this house that was written up in best-designed homes. I like that."

[Author note: Paradigms function in all areas of our lives. My own public relations paradigm, formed from the thought of "I want potential clients to feel comfortable hiring me," is evaluating this chapter at the moment with thoughts such as: "Gee – is it good for business to put this in? You said you would keep the book brief and now you are talking about stuff that's not in any design book I've seen. Plus, many clients use these paradigms and it may not make them feel good to have them spelled out in ways that might be considered unflattering. Get rid of this chapter and get on with publishing the book!!!!"

So why is the chapter still here? We have more than one paradigm. There's another thought that says: I want this book to deeply explore every important aspect of the design process, leading to the paradigm of "Book as a candid presentation of all aspects of landscaping," leads to thoughts such as: How exciting to be exploring a topic I've never seen in a design book that gets at the heart of why 80% of all gardens are fairly similar. Keep writing!!!]

Internally based thoughts that also lead to common paradigms include:

- I want to have fun with my family. (Creates the paradigm of "Landscape to provide family enjoyment.")
- I want to relax and have fun with retirement. (Creates the paradigm of "Landscaping to make me comfortable and relaxed.")

- I want a new hobby to keep me busy. (Creates the paradigm of "Landscaping as a way to stretch and grow.")

There are many other possible paradigms for creating a landscape that are far less common. I'll share several to give you a sense of how big the range is.

- I want to do something to celebrate the way I feel. (Leads to a paradigm of "Landscaping as a celebration of feelings."
- I want my entire property to be a sacred space and remind me that I am a sacred being. (Creates the paradigm of "Landscaping to express and remember my sacredness.")
- I want to create something completely original and unique on a grand scale. (Leads to the paradigm: "Landscaping as a canvas to express majestic uniqueness.")
- I want to make everyone laugh, smile and remember their childhood. (Leads to the paradigm of: "Landscaping as a source for humor, healing and Nostalgia.")
- I want to heal this disease I have. (Leads to the paradigm: "Landscape as a healing space.")
- I want to let all the world know that I believe in god. (Leads to the paradigm of: "Landscape as an altar to divinity.")
- I want to remember and honor the dead. (Leads to the paradigm: "Landscape as a memorial to honor the dead.")
- I want to become intimate with all the faces of self. (Leads to the paradigm: "Landscape as a canvas to express my many unique sides.")
- I want to celebrate the power of science. (Leads to the paradigm of: "Landscape as a space to reveal the power and beauty of science and innovation.)

- I want to create a sanctuary for biodiversity. (Leads to the paradigm: "Landscape as a wildlife refuge.")
- I want to create mystery, wonder and surprise. (Leads to the paradigm: "Landscape as treasure chest to be revealed.")

The biggest difference in a design paradigm shift is not necessarily in the external form of the landscape, although each of these different paradigms naturally shifts the way we evaluate and thus make each of the thousands of large and small choices that make up a landscape. The biggest difference is the way we feel and think about the landscape as we design, create, live in and maintain it. Because our consciousness processes information physically, emotionally and mentally 1/3rd of our experience is physical, and the other two thirds of our experience is mental and emotional. Because our landscape paradigms directly affect all our thoughts and feelings about our landscape they are arguably as important to US personally as the external shape the landscape takes.

The exploration and conscious choice of our landscape paradigms opens up a door to the most exciting possibilities within landscaping. Certainly a landscape is valuable as a tool for gaining neighborhood acceptance, but that is unlikely to be a peak experience. If, however, a landscape becomes something more: A vehicle for expressing devotion to a spouse, a healing sanctuary or a place to bring joy to an honored guest, it has a very real possibility of moving us as designers and creators into an arena of significance. Landscaping then becomes an art form to express something bigger than physical and social survival that can touch both us and others.

Creating a Healing Garden

A healing garden begins with the paradigm of landscape as a vehicle for healing. Healing in its most basic meaning refers to restoring well-being through balance and wholeness. Whatever has this impact is healing.

Creating a healing and sacred space can take many forms. For one person it might be a miniature village with model trains. For another it might be a swing among favorite scented plants. It can be filled with personal art and sculpture or a Zen garden, filled with simplicity. traditional and empty.

The form will change for each person because it's not about the form, but about the way WE feel about the form. A man who dreamed of having wonderful model trains as a child but was pushed by circumstances into quickly taking heavy responsibilities at a young age that precluded play, may find it enormously healing (balance and wholeness) to build an amazing model train set through a miniature garden. Another man, constantly forced to examine details at work that go against the strong broad sweeps of quick decisions that come naturally would find anything miniature in his recreational life frustrating. A tennis court or forgetting the garden altogether and going to the beach might be more healing. Healing is not something that can be boxed into somber or "spiritual" stereotypes. It often has a lot to do with FUN, and sometimes the most fun garden is one you don't have to think about, spend money on or maintain.

There are many ways a garden can be healing. One is through associative memories. For example, the first flower I remember growing up was a GORGEOUS grouping of purple peonies. When I saw a five gallon pot of Peonies the other day it brought a smile to my face so I bought it. This is why a healing garden is so personal. It's not about looking up what is a "healing plant" in some book. Our specific positive memories are a valuable resource to integrate into our garden because things that activate those memories will affect us more powerfully than things that have no memory attached.

A healing garden can either be own clearly defined areas within a larger garden or can be the entire garden. This applies not only to healing gardens but to any paradigm. The front garden might be dedicated to pleasing the neighbors, the back lawn and surrounding beds to pleasing a partner and kids, and the far back left garden to being a wildlife preserve, while the far back right garden is your personal healing garden.

Sometimes what is healing about the garden is creating it. There may or may not be any special theme or discernible results. But the fact that you personally brought balance by giving yourself permission to do whatever you want and personally DO the work helped you get in touch with an important part of who you are that is not expressed in the office or with friends.

I encourage you to start with the feeling you want your space to have or the feeling you want to have creating it. This is the feeling you want to feel when you spend time there. Then let images of plants, stone, water, color and sounds present themselves that for you carry the quality of this feeling. These images may be appropriate to translate literally into your landscape or not. If not, you can pick symbols of those pictures. If you imagine Niagara Falls you obviously can't build that. You could visit it. You could record it and pipe the sound into your healing garden. Or you could pick a fountain or waterfall that makes you think of the image.

Be aware that because a healing garden is primarily defined by your personal thoughts and feelings about it, inner dialog is more important than the result. The goal is not to create the PERFECT healing garden for sunset magazine, leading to stress about all the areas that "don't quite have the true Zen touch I was looking for!"

If you are a perfectionist who always worries about what others thinks, the perfect healing garden for you may be a weed patch and an old deck chair. Every day you can go and look at how the weeds are growing and notice what's different about the weeds today, without doing anything. You might observe the dilapidated deck chair and consider which bit of paint will fall off next, while reminding yourself that you are a great person whether or not you have a designer deck-chair. Of course you already know this logically, but healing is often about the parts of us that are not logical and have just as much impact on our daily life.

Carrying on with the perfectionist/weed-patch theme: It might be healing to bring your friends to your weed patch and tell them how you sit and watch weeds grow. Perhaps your perfectionism has intimidated them and your garden will help them laugh and heal imbalances in the relationship. Relationships are far more important than gardens so a garden that brings us closer to those we love becomes something really special, bringing us far more value than it costs.

And of course the opposite is true. If your whole life feels like a disheveled, out of control mess that you can't personally do much about right now, creating a bonsai garden with meticulous order may be the most fun and balancing thing you could do.

If healing for you is about deepening your connection to god (your definition for whatever is more than humanity and sacred), then working either with tradition or your personal intuition can bring another level to your healing garden. There are many ways of doing this on a practical level. Symbols can be chalked, painted, sand-blasted or carved into stone, glass or arranged in pebbles. Stain glass, vertical or horizontal, can be incorporated. I've always found crystals to be particularly beautiful visually and emotionally and have developed a variety of ways to bring those into a garden setting. You can look at some of my sculptures if you are drawn to crystals in the "Sacred Spaces" portion of www.MysticalLandscapes.com (I called the company that even though 90% of my work is traditional landscaping to alert people that a garden can also at times be mystical).

Consider creating an area in your garden that is just for this purpose. Do a Google search for "Mystical Gardens" or "Sacred Spaces" if you need ideas. And if you are a very mental person, healing may be in the form of turning off the brain that analyzes costs and design details and noticing if any image truly touches your heart and uplifts you.

Once you create your sacred space, spend time tending it any time you need renewal or want to experience a deeper connection with yourself. Much of what makes a space healing may go on in your mind, either in stillness, or in consciously directing your creative mind towards images, ideas and goals that inspire and excite you on a deep level.

Part Three:

Installing Your Landscape

Installing Your Landscape in Stages

There are several benefits to breaking your project into stages:

- It puts less strain on your short-term cash-flow.
- It may allow you to see some of your design installed and then refine your design for other areas, based on how you like stage one.
- It may be less disruptive to your life-style to have a break between projects.
- Neighbors and city/county officials may be less worried if you develop a large project incrementally.

The downside to doing things in stages often includes:

- There are two areas of inflation that affect landscaping. One is material prices, which go up an average of 4% per year. The other is codes and permits. Every year more things are regulated. For example, in the last few years irrigation systems that are newly installed are required to spend an extra $100.00 on what used to be a check valve assembly AND then have the new valve device inspected every year or so. The new device is less flexible so cost may be spent placing it in a location it will work. Net 100% increase in costs for that one area.
- Landscapes are typically more efficiently installed as a unit. For example, if you rent a trencher for the back yard and then rent it again for the front yard at a later date in order to lay irrigation pipe, you may pay twice as much as doing it all at the same time.
- Landscape companies may factor larger jobs with less profit margin than two or three smaller jobs to reflect the fact that they are more efficient to install. For example, I sometimes give clients doing more than $50,000.00 in work at one time a 10% discount to reflect the fact that

jobs of this size are often easier for me to manage and install than three $15,000.00 jobs, all of which need their own contract, clean up, meetings etc.

- You have to wait longer to enjoy your garden.
- Because large jobs get done with a bigger crew they are done in fewer working days than the same job broken up into stages. If the front yard can only hold about four people working without getting in each other's way that is the crew size I typically allocate. However, if the back-yard could also handle four people I might have six to eight people working rather than four for stage one and four for stage two. In this way the project might be done in half the working days, which can be nice if you find work done at your home disruptive.

Knowing how to break your design into efficient stages is one of those areas where an experienced installer can help you. The variables are too design and sit-specific to give a universal recipe here. However, I'll share general things to keep in mind.

Make a list of the things that are most important to you to get done based on your personal preference. It might look something like:

1) Make the front entrance area nice.
2) Put landscape lighting on the front walk.
3) Erect a dog fence.
4) Create a play area for the kids.
5) Transplant mother's roses out of the pots.

These are your personal priorities but are almost certainly not the most cost effective or efficient sequence for the work to be done in. This creates a tension in values between doing things in the order that will be most pleasing to you and saving the most money. So that you can make an educated decision in this area it is helpful to make a concrete comparison:

- Install the landscape in stages based on my ideal sequence will cost: $21,200.00
- Install the landscape in the most efficient stages will cost: $18,100.00
- Installing the landscape in one complete stage: $17,000.00

In this comparison you can see that you save $3,100.00 by breaking things down into the most efficient stages and save an additional $1,100.00 as a result of doing everything right now. You can then weigh whether the benefits of stretching your cash-flow from your ideal of doing three separate $7,000.00 stages over three years and having to wait three years for the garden to feel complete outweighs the benefits of having things finished now with a $4,100.00 savings.

Why does the sequence of things affect the price so much? Going back to the list above that is based on your ideal sequence and priorities, here is a likely scenario:

- The dog fencing will likely be more efficient if it is installed as the last thing so that work-traffic does not have to deal with the fence.
- The back-yard will likely be done easier if the crew does not have to be careful with the entrance landscape that you want to do first.
- The dog fence will be more efficient if tied in with other carpentry, such as trellis, benches and deer fencing.
- The landscape lighting wires and transformers can best be laid and chosen for the entire garden simultaneously.
- The clean-up cycle for two stages can be eliminated with just one clean-up at the end.
- Transplanting the roses requires bringing the tiller in to rototill just one area. If the whole area is tilled and not planted weeds will grow. Perhaps bagged soil needs to

be brought in rather than the efficiency of one dump-truck load of soil for the entire back garden and one trip with the tiller, followed by comprehensive planting and mulching.

- The play-structure may be in the way of the ideal trench-path for irrigation lines that come later.

Here are some general guidelines for breaking a project down into stages with the least amount of additional cost:

1) Breaking a project down by large area, such as the entire front yard and the entire back-yard is often ideal.
2) Doing the back-yard first so that all equipment/traffic/materials can be brought easily through the front yard before it is landscaped is ideal.
3) Doing things in the following order is ideal:
    a. Develop an overall design, even if you won't be installing it all at once.
    b. Remove and demo the old/ consider what might be incorporated into the grading stage (concrete pieces can be buried etc. if heavy equipment is used for grading).
    c. Grade all soil.
    d. Build all hardscapes, including walls, ponds, stairs, paths, benches, fences etc.
    e. Spread chicken manure and rototill all soil.
    f. Lay irrigation infrastructure so that mail lines go to all beds and the controller/timer/valves are set up for the whole property.
    g. Buy drip irrigation materials and install all lawn spray heads.
    h. Install mole deterring mesh below lawn.
    i. Install any sod and turn on zones controlling the sod.

j. Buy all plants and set out prior to planting for design refinement.
k. Plant all plants.
l. Immediately add drip irrigation to all plantings and turn on those valves to water new plantings.
m. Install any low-voltage lighting.
n. Spread bark/mulch on all planting beds between plants within three days of planting to cut down on weed seed germination by 30%.
o. Spread gravel or top off gravel on all paths.
p. Do final clean up on full area.

This is typically the ideal sequence to do things in. Using this sequence can increase efficiency by an average of 20%, which is huge when applied to an entire landscape. If things are broken into stages this is still a great sequence to apply. The back can be done following this sequence and then the front. Or the front and back can be done up to the point where the hardscape is complete. Then the next stage can be soil amending, planting etc.

What Time of Year to Install?

I'll begin by providing you with some context:

- Plants love to be transplanted or planted in low light, moist soil and regular rain (i.e. Winter).
- The best time to seed wildflowers or start drought-tolerant plants that won't have an irrigation system is as soon as the fall rains begin in earnest.
- Some soils, particularly heavy clay soil, become exponentially more difficult to rototill, grade, drive equipment in and shovel when they are wet – and even more so if it is raining while the work is going on.

Most gardens have a mix of hardscaping and planting. So in the winter my planting is easy and I don't need to baby and hand water things every day until the irrigation system is installed. In the summer I have to fuss with new plantings but don't have to walk around with shoes caked with mud or wash my hands every few minutes so as not to get power-tools muddy. It's obviously a lot more fun to install when it's dry.

One technique if you are doing major grading during the winter in heavy soil is to use large tarps or plastic (be sure and weight this down with heavy weights every ten feet) and only remove this and work on dry days. This is particularly important if heavy equipment is involved.

In summary:

- If you are worried about moving plants and don't have a green thumb, plant in fall or winter.
- If you have lots of free time at a certain point and want to garden, make the best of it.
- If you hate foul weather, do the job when you enjoy it.
- If you can, hardscape in the summer.

Using the Right Tools

Using great tools is fun! It makes things go smoothly with less effort and frustration. As a professional, it always pays to have the best tools. As a do-it-yourself home-owner doing one project you need to weigh things, such as:

- Will I have a use for this tool after the project is done?
- How many hours will this tool save me and how much does it cost?
- Could I easily resell this tool after the project is done?
- Do I enjoy nice tools whether they are a profitable investment or not?

The basics you will need:

- Square and pointed shovel
- Pick
- Six foot digging bar
- Comfortable gloves
- Screw-driver
- Hammer
- Saw
- Sledge hammer
- Rake
- Soil tamper
- Rototiller (rental for big flat areas, mini tiller for steep slopes)
- Irrigation tool kit including pipe-cutter
- 3' landscape rake
- Well-made wheelbarrow

It will be best if your tools have strong fiberglass handles, both so they break under pressure or rot when the wooden handles get wet. There are other tools that can be very helpful in some situations:

- An extension ladder.
- A small chainsaw with several spare chains.
- An 18volt Battery Tool-kit with at least four batteries including
  - Two drills/screwdrivers
  - A hammer drill for concrete
  - A sawsall with a good assortment of blades
  - An angle grinder with metal and masonry blades
  - A circular saw
  - A sander
- A pressure washer
- An air powered nail gun and stapler with compressor and 50' of hose
- An extension cord long enough to reach to the corner of your property from the closest outlet
- A machete
- A large two-handed pruner
- An assortment of nails, screws, washers etc.
- A 4' level with a built in laser

Some examples of where the right tool really makes a difference:

- A 14" very sharp blade on a sawsall can root-prune bamboo and also thin out some of the canes significantly faster and neater than anything else.
- When positioning boulders a top-of-the-line solid-core fiberglass shovel can both dig the hole to sink the boulders in (makes them look more natural) and serve as a crow bar to lever the rocks into place.
- A plastic garbage can slung over the back can be a great way to take large quantities of soil or mulch up or down steps.

- When putting in a deck having two drills, one with the deck-screw bit and the other with the drill-bit saves a lot of time over switching out the bits constantly.
- Using a laser level to predict water-surface on a far bank when constructing a pond is critical.
- Using a steel-cutting blade on an angle grinder to cut away the metal fencing used to contain palletized rock can speed up the process considerably on large deliveries of palletized rock.
- Using an excavator with a blade and thumb for large grading, stump removal, concrete demo or burying things can do the work of eight or more laborers with less hassle.
- Using a pick to trench not only saves time but means less soil is disturbed.

I was recently given the job of demolishing a ten foot concrete cube. I'd never demolished concrete so thick before. Faced with a potentially grueling process I went on YouTube to search for options. I found one that worked beautifully using a product I had never heard of. In other words, when you are doing something big and unfamiliar, it's a good idea to watch someone else do it well – and the internet is a great place to start for free.

Maintaining Good Neighbor Relations

A neighbor can be a valuable partner in your landscape project in several ways:

- Providing access through their property to yours for certain types of equipment or deliveries.
- Support around permits that may be needed.
- Cooperation around parking in tight neighborhoods.
- Joint-planning and/or payment of projects along the property line including:
  o Shared fences.
  o Jointly designed plantings that compliment both sides.
  o Drainage issues.
  o House-painting color coordination.
  o Deer management (as in not needing to put up a deer fence between your properties if a perimeter fence goes around both your properties).

The best way to maintain good neighbor relations is to voluntarily include them in the process or to share the plan with them before work begins. In addition it is important to minimize negative impacts from the project on neighbors, which can include:

- Noise at crucial times.
- Shocking noise for infants or pets.
- Dust during construction.
- Contractor taking up their parking spaces.
- Fear of the unknown.
- Blocking their view in some way.
- Destroying some of their privacy.
- Construction music.
- Cars scratched by delivery trucks.

Having a conversation with your contractor before a contract is signed about these things can be a good idea. For example, if you know your neighbor has a sleeping child at 2pm and one construction approach involves bringing in jack hammers and another involves resurfacing existing concrete or doing something more time-consuming by hand, you might ask your contractor how much more money it would cost to do a quieter approach. If there is a $300.00 dollar difference in price you have the information to either make your decision or approach your neighbor and say "If you would prefer a silent construction process you are welcome to pay my contractor $300.00 and she will do more of the work by hand than normal." It's not fair to the contractor to accept a bid and then request that they use less efficient means of installing the work.

Landscape Resources I Use

Below is a quick overview of the main landscape resources I use and why. I considered not including this because some suppliers may consider it to show uninformed favoritism (and not stock a book that ignores them or seems critical) and other readers may be disappointed that their neighborhood stores are not represented. I've included it anyway, with all of its subjectivity because it could be useful to you, as it is to me in my daily shopping for my jobs. Because 80% of my work has been in Mill-Valley and I live in San Rafael there are many suppliers in Fairfax, Novato etc. where I have not even visited (do write in and tell me if you know them well and perhaps I'll include those in a future edition of the book).

This is not meant to be an objective review of all Marin suppliers. What it will tell you is most of what I have needed to buy everything I have needed for my projects in the Bay Area. Below each of the suppliers I share my reasons for shopping and not shopping there.

Be sure and check out the coupon chapter of the book to find some great ways to save money at a few of my personal favorite places!

Retail Plants: (Wholesale plants are not available to home-owners so I'll only mention retailers here.)

- Home Depot, San Rafael: 111 Shoreline Pkwy.
  - Pros:
    - Low retail prices
    - Good quantity selection (30 plants or more of most varieties)
    - Decent plants
    - Good warranty
  - Cons:

- Poor service and unknowledgeable staff.
- Long lines.
- Hard to special order anything.
- Erratic stocking of plants with no number to call to find out what's in stock.

- Green Jeans Garden Supply, Mill Valley: 690 Redwood Highway. Phone: 415- 389-8333
  - Pros: Good variety of unusual plants.
    - Very knowledgeable staff.
    - High quality plants.
    - Easy to special-order.
    - Short lines.
  - Cons:
    - Low quantities: (1-15 plants for most plants)
    - High prices.

- Sloats Garden Center, Multiple Locations:
  - Pros:
    - Reasonable quantities (5-20 on most plants)
    - Some of the staff is very knowledgeable
    - Good quality plants.
    - Very easy to special order.
    - A number of locations.
  - Cons:
    - High prices.
    - Often a short wait in lines.

Rock, Soil and Bark:

- American Soil and Stone, San Rafael: #A 565 Jacoby St. Phone: 415-456-1381
  - Pros:

- Best selection of products in Marin.
- Lowest prices for products I use last time I compared them.
- Interesting art/sculpture in the yard.
- Reasonable service.
- Good fork-lift.
- You can return used pallets.

  o Cons:

  - Be careful not to hit a boulder in their parking lot.
  - Some of the drivers are not the most experienced and as a result they may not want to put things in spots that are little tight but would be fine for a driver with more experience.
  - It's a good idea to look under any truck for leaking oil if you have a nice driveway and are worried about that.

- Shamrock Materials, San Rafael: 548 DuBois St. Phone: 415-455-1575

  o Pros:

  - They have the best forklift around for getting things up steep hills
  - All drivers I've used are very experienced.
  - No oil leaks on trucks.
  - Very professional staff.
  - An OK selection of materials.

  o Cons:

  - Prices are about 10% higher than American Soil and they have less than half the selection as American Soils.
  - It is hard to get through to their dispatcher to reschedule or check on things and the phone system is a bit complicated (expect to wait and/or leave unreturned messages

– good news is they usually listen to messages and do what is asked).
- Often takes a few days to get a delivery.

Tool Rentals:

- Tam Valley Rentals: 240 Shoreline Hwy, Mill Valley Phone: 415-383-7311
  o Pros:
    - Nicest owners I have ever met.
    - Very reasonable prices.
    - Helpful and knowledgeable staff.
    - Rent the Barreto tiller I like.
  o Cons:
    - Very limited supply of rental tools.

- Hertz Equipment Rentals, Corte Madera: 5764 Paradise Dr. Phone: 415-924-4444
  o Pros:
    - Can order in most of what you might want.
    - Reasonable selection of materials.
    - Tools in very good condition.
  o Cons:
    - The rental process is a bit cumbersome.
    - Expect to wait 5-15 minutes.
    - They have removed the thumbs from many of their excavators (thumbs are critical for landscaping with an excavator).
    - Prices on the high side.

- All Star Rents, San Rafael: 501 Dubois St. Phone: 415-453-6940
  o Pros:
    - Minimal wait time.
    - Decent prices.
    - Can rent the Barreto tiller I like.

- Can get excavator with thumb.
  - o Cons:
    - Tools are sometimes rented out in poor condition and break.

Hardware:

- Goodman's Ace Hardware, Mill Valley: 775 Redwood Hwy. Phone: 415-388-6233
  - o Pros:
    - GREAT one-stop shop.
    - Low cost on many tools.
    - Fairly knowledgeable staff with plenty of people to help.
    - Short lines.
    - Easy detour on 101.
    - Open until 7pm.
    - Friendly staff.
    - Easy to find things.
    - Easy parking.
  - o Cons:
    - None that I can think of.

- Home Depot, San Rafael: 111 Shoreline Pkwy.
  - o Pros:
    - Open until 9pm.
    - The Ryobi brand of cordless tools in their kits are the cheapest way to get reasonable cordless tools. One battery fits thirty different cordless tools.
    - Cement, lumber and a few other things are the cheapest.
    - Able to find most things in one stop.
    - Cheap selection of low-voltage lighting kits.
    - Good quantities of most things.

- o Cons:
    - Service is often terrible with long waits to ask questions, wait in line, or get help loading.
    - The quality is often very poor on products.
    - Hard to find what you need/want.
    - Easy to waste time looking for things that could easily be found in a smaller store.

- OSH, San Rafael: 1151 Andersen Dr.
  Phone: 415-453-7288
    - o Pros:
        - Open until 9pm.
        - Great selection of basic tools on sale in their tool bins.
        - Low costs on everything.
        - Half the hassle of parking and finding things as Home Depot.
        - Reasonably knowledgeable service.
        - Low wait times.
        - Landscape materials are loaded into your car/truck easily and quickly.
    - o Cons:
        - Plant nursery has very limited quantity.
        - Does not have a GREAT selection of some things, such as irrigation and lighting products and some tools.

Water Features:

- Water Savers Irrigation, San Rafael. 508 Irwin St.
  Phone: 415-454-6581
    - o I have not used them enough to give a list of pros and cons. They do have a good selection of lawn edging materials, irrigation supplies and can order

sod. They have some water-feature materials as well.

- Urban Farmer, Mill Valley (see irrigation)
- Amazon, Online (see online). Amazon may be the cheapest place to buy a pump if you know exactly what you need.

Irrigation:

- Urban Farmer, Mill Valley: 653 E. Blithedale Ave.
  Phone: 415-380-3840
    - o Pros:
        - Very well staffed with knowledgeable people.
        - GREAT selection of odds and ends.
        - Willing to help you map out your own irrigation system and design (the only place that does this).
        - Has low-voltage lights and bulbs as well.
        - Will loan out low-voltage light kit at no charge so you can see the effect before buying the fixtures.
        - Has a decent selection of water-feature pumps and accessories.
    - o Cons:
        - For the non-professional (I get a good discount) their prices will be high – sometimes the highest around (though some of their drip products are cheaper than Home-Depot).
    - o Summary: Unless you know what you are doing, pay the higher price in materials (cheap) to avoid mistakes (expensive) and get great, prompt service.

Landscape Lighting:

- See Home Depot, Hardware
- See Urban Farmer, Irrigation.
- See Amazon, Online.

Online:

- Google Search under "Shopping" Tab:
  - Pros:
    - Great prices.
    - You can sometimes find things that are not locally available.
    - Easy to compare prices.
    - Easy to see pictures to know if it is what you want.
  - Cons:
    - Many things don't show up in the search.
    - Easy to describe things sometimes don't show up but if you asked your local hardware store they would direct you to a product in a minute.
    - Not easy to return things in many cases.
    - Some risk when giving money to unknown sources.

- Amazon With Prime Membership (prime costs $70.00 per year):
  - Pros:
    - Best customer review system I have seen!
    - One-click ordering (once you know what you want all you have to do is click your mouse once and most items will be shipped for free within two days to your home using your card on file).

- Decent search ability.
- Able to sell things as well.
- Better prices in many instances than local stores even after shipping.
- Get things in 24 hours for only $3.99 in shipping.
- Easy to read/navigate the page.
- They have MANY things, from fencing to water-feature materials to lighting etc.
- Free instant-streaming movies for prime-members.
- A reasonable return policy.

o Cons:

- Not all things are cheaper than at a local store. This is particularly true for heavy, bulky items.
- You sometimes need to know the model number or it won't come up in the search.
- They may sell the same thing three times in separate areas of the site at different prices.
- No one to ask a question not addressed in the sometimes limited descriptions: "Will this switch work on fluorescent lights?"

Debris Boxes:

I have used both Grange Debris, which services all of Marin and Mill Valley Refuse, which last time I checked had a narrower delivery range. In all cases Debris boxes pose a risk to nice driveways in the form of tire marks, scratches where the steel touches the concrete and in some cases oil leaks. I had a bad experience with Grange this past year that left me realizing that if I wanted to be sure to avoid marks I would have to be very proactive. The owner, Fred Grange, came by and agreed to clear up the tire marks and oil stains, and said he will be implementing a better communication format to prepare customers on what to expect. I've never had any problem with Mill Valley Refuse but think that it's good to be on the safe side. Three sheets of plywood and a prior conversation with the dispatcher are minimum precautions needed to safeguard your driveway if you are worried about scratches. All boxes and trucks vary so you will need to request instructions on how to prepare the space and possibly send an e-mail photo to be sure.

In general debris boxes are a great asset on large projects for disposing of excess materials. Both companies have one kind of box exclusively for dirt, concrete or asphalt and another for yard waste and all other garbage. Sizes range from 4 yards to 40 yards and cost around $130.00 and up per delivered and picked up box, depending on the size.

San Rafael and Mill Valley Refuse, which services Mill Valley and

Bonus Section #1

Part Four:

Successfully Working with Professionals

Should you Hire a Professional?

Here are some reasons to consider hiring a professional:

- A reliable crew will get the work done 3-10 times faster than you will, working alone.
- A knowledgeable crew will do a decent to excellent job and probably provide you with a one year warranty.
- A good designer will likely save you more money by avoiding mistakes, increasing your property value and expanding your options than the design costs.
- If you don't enjoy gardening this frees up your time to do things you enjoy more.
- It can be exciting to watch your vision become a reality quickly.
- If you are not conditioned to hard work, it is quite common for you to strain or sprain something that costs you more in medical bills and/or time off work than the money saved by doing it yourself.

Reasons not to hire a professional include:

- If it's a job you can easily do and it would be simpler to just do it than go through the hassle of interviewing, negotiating a contract, explaining what you want and then waiting for them to be available for your job.
- If you need to save money and have experience in the area you can probably cut the cost in half.
- If you know what you are doing and want something done with exceptional quality and detailing it is sometimes hard to find a contractor who is capable and willing to do the work with the level of artistry and detail that you would do yourself.
- If you need to be personally involved on a daily basis to make sure things are going the way you want them to

and if it takes you a while to make up your mind. A contractor cannot profitably stop or slow-down beyond their normal pace. In this case you are best working alone or perhaps with one knowledgeable assistant, handyman.

- If you can use the exercise inherent in installing landscape and would enjoy it.
- You are bored and want the challenge of learning something new.

Professional Options to Consider

Professionals come in a number of varieties. I'll describe the pros/cons of each and you can make sure that the professional you choose contains the list of ingredients you seek:

English-speaking or not:

There is a good percentage of the immigrant labor force, mostly Spanish that does not speak English well. This may not be a problem if you speak their language or the work is simple and mistakes will not cost you much, particularly if you are supervising and can show them physically what needs to be done. Non-English speaking labor is typically 30% less expensive, reflecting supply and demand.

Legal resident or not:

About half of the Hispanic and non-English speaking labor is not working legally. They may be here as a visitor or they may have entered the country illegally. This precludes many of the options below relating to licenses and insurance.

Is your professional licensed?

A license costs around $200.00 per year and requires that you maintain a bond. Any licensed professional landscaper will have a bond that provides you with about $12,000.00 in security if your contractor does not finish the job or do the work in accordance with the contract. In other words, if your licensed contractor took the money you had paid them and left the job part-way through, you could probably get around $12,000.00 from their bond company, minus any legal expenses. The license simply means the contractor has paid the state and passed a very basic written test using multiple choice questions. Which means it's not accurate to assume that someone licensed knows a lot or that someone who is not licensed does not know anything.

Does your professional carry general liability insurance?

From the home-owners perspective this can be a more important variable than whether or not your contractor is licensed. Landscapers are not legally required to have general liability policies. This typically covers things like damage to your building by the contractor, fire etc. Like most insurance policies, they focus on the lump sum: "This is a two million dollar policy!" But when it gets right down to it they may only have an allowance for $50,000.00 if the contractor burns down your house by accident or drops a tree on it. Still, this is a lot better than nothing and may be important, depending on the details of your home-owner's policy. It is considerably more important if your contractor is operating heavy equipment, cutting trees or building retaining walls than it is if your contractor is helping you plant one gallon plants with a shovel.

Does your contractor have health insurance?

This relates to accidents on the job. It is more likely that a serious accident would occur with someone using a chainsaw, circular saw, heavy equipment, jack-hammer etc. than if they plant a plant, but the reality remains that we can get injured any time any place.

The sole proprietor of a company can carry health insurance, such as Kaiser, which also covers them on the job. Coverage for subcontractors and employees is separate. Subcontractors need to have their own insurance to be covered and employees must have "work-man's comprehensive." This insures that an employee on the job that is injured will receive medical treatment that is paid for by the workman's comp. policy and in some cases the worker may receive disability and/or retraining. Without this, they are typically taken to the emergency room where they receive emergency treatment that the hospital is not reimbursed for because this would typically be an immigrant worker who may or may not be legally here and who has no money. In other cases the employer and/or home-owner might be sued for medical expenses.

Does your contractor charge sales tax?

Labor is not taxed. Materials are. When labor and materials are combined in a contract labor becomes taxed and materials that are marked up become taxed at the higher rate. If your contractor gives you fixed-bid contracts rather than time and material estimates it will typically add 5% to the total cost of the job in the form of increased taxes (though this is typically more than absorbed in cost-overruns that abound in time and material contracts).

Does your contractor offer design/build service?

Design and build companies offer several key advantages over design-only and build-only companies:

- In a small company you may work with just one person, who becomes more accountable and with whom you develop more of a relationship.
- As a result you avoid the scenario where the designer tells you it will cost one price and be fine and the installer tells you he does not recommend that approach and, by the way, it will cost twice what the designer said.
- People who install landscapes are often more sensitive to costs and practicality when they design.

On the flip side, being an installer in no way implies design talent or intelligence. Asking an installer "what do you think," without first verifying the installer's design skills is a very common mistake home-owners make.

Choosing a Designer

I recommend that you choose a landscape designer to help you with your project even if you create your own design. I did this myself when I designed and built my first custom home and landscape. I discovered that the hardest design I had ever done was for me.

Sometimes it is hard to make up our mind in a vacuum and two fresh minds are often better than one. What I did, and what I suggest you do, is after I had developed my basic overall concept I brought in a colleague to review them with me and then listened to the feedback he gave me. In my case I mostly continued to do what I had planned to do. However, I incorporated a few of his ideas and the process left me feeling clearer and more confident that I was doing the right thing. All that for a few hours of his time.

Picking your landscape designer may be the most important decision you make in your entire project. Why? Because a great idea may take only half an hour to develop but that one idea could save you hundreds or thousands of dollars while helping you realize more of your goals and values than another idea that cost more. In short you will spend less money and time and ideas than on any other aspect of the project but the quality of those ideas will determine ALL of the value you receive for your entire investment. It is not at all uncommon to see $10,000 spent on some project that needs to be redone for $15,000 in a few years because it was poorly thought out. In some cases it costs as much to demolish a mistake as it does to do it right the first time so you end up paying three times: First to install a mistake, then to undo it, and finally to do it right.

No matter the cost, pick the very best designer you can find, relative to your personal values to either review your existing design or work with you to develop a new one. In some cases it even makes sense to work with a great designer to develop your design and then have your next best choice review that design before implementing it. This 1-2 hour review will be well worth it if it leads to even ONE improved or totally new idea that you like or which saves you money.

Here are different things to consider when choosing a designer:

- How soon can they start your design process?

- What are their design fees?

- If you don't like the direction things are going in after the first few hours can you bow out and just pay for those hours or are you locked in?

- Are they someone you like and enjoy talking with?

- Are they able to fit into your ideal daily routine?

- A designer who has background as an installer will be able to design more practically and efficiently than a designer whose primary experience and expertise is on paper. This can save you thousands of dollars in lower bids when you have your design installed.

- The quality of a designer's listening skills and their ability to understand clearly what you want will make the difference between the first design hitting the bull's eye or taking two or three revisions to finally design what you want. As each revision costs money a designer with great communication skills can easily cut your design costs in half!

- A designer who thinks intelligently outside the box can recognize unique opportunities to give you what you want in original ways that work well on your particular site. This skill can save you hundreds, thousands or even tens of thousands of dollars in some instances.

- A designer who is well resourced and knows who sells what at what cost can design more efficiently and hit the target budget more accurately.

- A designer who has extensive knowledge of plants, diseases, deer resistance etc. can help you design more elaborate and distinctive plantings that look good both short and long-term.

- A designer with a good balance of left/right brain skills will be able to design a highly creative and beautiful design that is functional to live in, hits your budget and is easy to maintain.

- A licensed landscape architect has an added bonus of being able to "stamp" their own drawings. What this means is that in some areas of engineering you will not need to hire a separate engineer to review your designer's drawings. This can save money and allow more creativity when doing large-scale projects that require permits.

- A designer that also installs the work can help you in several ways:

  o The design drawings will not need to be as extensive when the designer is installing the work because they know what they have designed and can install it as intended without a detailed to scale planl. As detailed drawings often represent more than HALF of the cost of a design, this savings allows you to spend more money on the landscape itself.

  o When the designer is also the installer there is more accountability around cost. It is not at all uncommon for landscape designers who do not install to do a design and tell the client "you should be able to install it for this amount." But in reality a designer who will not be giving a bid cannot know what other contractors will bid their design at. If on the other hand they say "You should be able to do this for this amount" and then give a bid themselves, if that bid is higher than quoted and the design needs to be redone to accommodate your budget you may be able to negotiate either a lower installation price or a no-cost revision of the design to fit your budget.

o A designer who installs your work will continue to fine-tune the design, often at no charge, as installation progresses. This makes for a more refined finished project.

o If you do change your mind about anything during the installation process and your installer designed the project it will be easy to revise the design on the spot. Otherwise you may need to call a meeting with the designer AND installer and pay the designer for the change or risk the change feeling inconsistent with the rest of the design.

o If you don't like what you get in the end it is not uncommon for a separate designer and installer to blame one another for the result. If they are the same person you have more accountability with that one person. Some designers offer project management but you will typically need to pay more for this service. When the designer is installing their own work you get this management for FREE!

Don't be afraid to spend money with a good designer. In my experience design is the most under-valued aspect of a landscape for many home-owners and it is paradoxically the most important. A few hundred dollars with the right person before you invest thousands installing a poorly thought-out idea can be the best money you ever spent. When it comes time to resell a design tailored to add property value can add significantly more value to a home than the project cost. A poorly thought-out design may even DETRACT from the property value and cost the same to install.

When interviewing a designer it can be helpful to:

- See their work in person and/or in pictures.

- Ask the designer how much experience they have installing and what resources they have for their materials.

- Talk with clients to see:
  - Did the design hit the budget target?

  - Did the designer listen and understand the client's values rather than push their own agenda?

  - Did the project perform as intended?

  - Was the designer available to participate in any last-minute revisions/changes that came up during installation?

In short, do your homework to insure you are picking the best designer for you and then benefit from their considerable expertise and experience.

Note: Over the years I've met many people that want to skip the design phase altogether because THEY DON'T HAVE VERY MUCH MONEY. This is when a design is MOST important.

When you have lots of money to spend it may even be fun to make mistakes and last minute changes that cost money. But when you are on a tight budget YOU CANNOT AFFORD to waste money on poorly thought out ideas. Designs do not need to be expensive, just well thought out.

Choosing an Installer

Every contractor brings a unique mix of skills and qualities to the table. No two contractors are alike. The relationship will be a good one if you take the time to clarify what you want out of the relationship and then pick a contractor that is strong in your top three priorities. Keep in mind that it is unlikely you will find a contractor who is strong in ALL areas so the important thing is focusing in on three or four areas that are most important to YOU.

Here is a list of strengths to consider:

- Able to start work right away.

- Lowest price.

- Best workmanship.

- Full attention on your project (work done quickly once begun).

- Clear and detailed communication.

- Calls you back and delivers requested information.

- Courteous and respectful around you.

- Good follow through - will do what they say.

- Calm and re-assuring presence.

- Fun to talk to and be around.

- Works hours that work well for your daily routine.

- Pleasant and safe around your children and pets.

- Extremely knowledgeable in areas relating to the project.

- Flexible and able/willing to accommodate your last-minute needs and/or requests.

- Comfortable doing the work while you are away so you don't need to be there.

- Open to you participating in the project so that you can:

  o Save money doing some of the work yourself.

  o Get exactly what you want.

  o Enjoy being involved in detailed decisions.

- Able to make a good connection with your neighbors.

- A large crew (work will be done quicker).

- Good accident liability protection in the form of:

  o General liability insurance.

  o Licensed and bonded.

  o Workman's comp for employees.

- Heavy equipment expertise (work will be done quicker and possibly for less money).

- An excellent warranty on all work done.

- Gives fixed costs so there are no surprises.

- Other:

Rank each of these on a 1-10 scale to indicate how important each of these qualities is to you. Your highest numbers are the things to focus on when interviewing a landscape contractor. Aim to find a contractor who is strong in the top three or four benefits you value most. If they are also strong in other areas important to you then celebrate your good fortune!

For example, if you want to find someone who begins and completes work when they say they do, don't focus on whether or not they are cheerful and make you feel comfortable. Instead ask them how many of their jobs in the last year began and ended when agreed. If their answer is acceptable, request phone numbers to talk to those clients and verify that the work was in fact done on time. If nine out of ten jobs were done on time and early there is a good chance you will be very happy in this area.

Keep in mind that it is YOUR responsibility to choose a contractor who will make YOU happy based on your values. Sometimes we assume that everyone values what WE value and don't ask friends or references the right questions. "Were you happy with the experience of hiring John Miller?" will get a different answer from different people because while John Miller ALWAYS does low-cost, low quality work and is always a bit late, the client who values saving money and does not have a deadline will like John and the client that wants quality workmanship and has a deadline will be terribly disappointed. In other words it DOES NOT MATTER how much other clients like or did not like the experience of working with your contractor, what matters is that the contractor you pick is strong in the areas that are important to you. Because if they are you will be very happy and get exactly what you want.

Having Your Project Done On Time

Projects are typically done late, both by contractors and home-owners. In the case of home-owners it is often a lack of external deadlines, biting off more than they can handle and a lack of focus and motivation amidst the many distractions at home. In the case of contractors it can be a mix of things:

- Contractor over-promising to try and please the client and/or get the job.

- Client indecisiveness or lack of timely communication at a key decision point.

- Contractor assuming the client will make their needs known and client assuming the contractor will ask them and delays resulting when these needs surface in mid project.

- Contractor doing more than one job at a time and experiencing a change on one of their other jobs.

- Weather.

- Delayed materials.

- Underestimating the time needed for the job.

- Crew unreliability.

- Equipment trouble or rental company out of a tool.

- An unreliable sub-contractor who's work must be done first for other work to proceed.

- A lack of incentive to finishing on time and a high incentive to take on other work from new clients who will not wait.

As the lowest bidder on a project can rarely afford to hire the best crew or buy reliable vehicles and equipment there is a natural tension between saving the most money and having your project done on time. It is good to decide which is more important to you. In addition the following steps will increase the likelihood of your job being done on time when hiring a contractor:

- Be patient and thorough in your design process. If there is not a detailed design it is impossible to accurately estimate the time things will take and easy to overlook necessary details. By starting with a clear and well-thought – out design most time-absorbing change-orders can be avoided.

- Ask your contractor for a list of all the decisions you will need to make throughout the project UP FRONT. Go over these, make as many as you can at the beginning and deliver this information in writing to your contractor. This means you cannot be used as an excuse for delays and adds a level of accountability to a contractor that lets them know you are serious about moving things along.

- Agree on a set deadline for work to be complete in writing.

- Add a penalty and/or incentive for work being done early. This could be financial or in the form of a promised good reference contingent on work being done early.

- Work with an integrated design and installation company. This will speed up the communication loop between designer, client and installer.

- Pick a company that does one job at a time with full attention until complete. It is far more likely that your job will be done on time if your contractor is not juggling other client's wishes, mistakes, requests and changes as well as your own.

- Ask your contractor to prepare a written time-table showing the sequence and schedule of work. This will not only encourage your contractor to give more thought to what is a realistic schedule, it will allow you to track if things are getting behind and stay in communication.

- Insure that a large sum of money will be paid when EVERYTHING is done and not before (this is done at the contract negotiation point).

- Inspect the work daily and let the contractor know RIGHT AWAY if something is not to your liking. This helps your contractor save time, proceed with confidence and rapidly adjust anything you don't like before the next stage of installation. Knowing you will be happy at the end increases most contractors' motivation to complete. If they can tell you are unhappy but don't speak up it creates a worrisome unknown that some contractors will avoid by focusing more on other clients.

- Praise your contractor when they are making good progress and communicate that the schedule is important.

Easy Rapport with Your Installer

Comfort: The "people factor" is very important to some people and if you are one of them it needs to be considered. Particularly if you are focused on quality of life and will be home during a long construction process, half the fun may be having enjoyable conversations with the crew. This can be determined by spending a little time with the contractor and/or asking to meet their crew while working on another job.

Clear, Accountable Communication: There are several ways to measure this:

- How often do you need to repeat yourself or remind your designer and/or contractor about what you want?

- Does your contractor do what they say they will in the areas that matter to you?

- When they don't do they take responsibility for the impact and make it up to you in some way?

There are several things that can be done to insure clear, accountable communication:

- Give your contractor/designer language to include in their contract. For example, if you don't want your new hose used as part of the construction process, ask that this be included in the contract and that any other things borrowed or used will be replaced with new items before final payment.

- When possible, pick a landscape company that has one contact person for all communication relating to both design and installation. This way you will only need to say things once and that one person is fully accountable to deliver as promised.

- Make any requests that are important to you in writing. These can be e-mailed or handed to your contractor. Be aware that if you make additional requests AFTER signing a contract that involve your contractor doing more work or doing the existing work with greater difficulty there will probably be an additional charge or it will create resentment in the relationship or slow things down. For example if the easiest way to the work-area is bringing materials by the front door and you request that your contractor carry them in a much longer way after they give you a bid this may add several hours to the construction process and require the bid to be adjusted accordingly.

Exceptional Workmanship

The quality of workmanship is determined not only by the skill of the crew, but by the specs in the contract. The quality of the work being done can be a huge variable in determining the price so to be sure that you will be happy it is good to show your contractor an example of how you want your work to look in an actual landscape and then see that this sample is referenced in your contract. This can be a "safer" approach for a home-owner who may not be able to visualize a contract spec. such as "flagstone to have an average of 1" gaps between them and be irregular." If instead the contract reads: "flagstone to exactly match the sample shown in Mrs. Smith's garden" there is little room for misunderstanding because you can walk over their at the end of the job and verify that it looks similar.

Durability: One aspect of quality workmanship is how long it will last without needing major maintenance. This is often in conflict with keeping costs down. For example, you can set sandstone in sand for half the of Three Rivers flagstone. However, it will not only start to crumble in time but the sandstone will lose its color and develop gray spots on it that look like mold. Using Three River's flagstone will always hold its color, never crumble and is several times more expensive to buy.

One way to insure that things have the durability you would like is to communicate with your designer about how long you want things to last and learn about the costs involved with meeting your goals. If you are doing something for a wedding and don't care much about the garden you may want to save money doing things that won't last more than a few months or years. If you are doing something that will be hard to replace and you don't like fussing with something ever once it's done the quality may need to be quite high, along with the price. The thing to be aware of is that there is no absolute quality level to always use, as quality affects your cost, maintenance, hassle, schedule and other things that may or may not be more important to you. To compare bids it is important that both bids refer to similar quality, otherwise you could choose to work with a slightly cheaper landscaper whose work was half the quality of another landscaper who would have been able to come in even lower if the quality levels were the same.

Low Maintenance: There are some things that save so much time and money in maintenance that they are cheaper within a matter of months or years than another cheaper approach. Using a Trex-type decking material that lasts years without any maintenance, staining or painting is one example.

Knowing Yourself: The most important thing is for you to know what you want and understand the various costs involved in having it. You may find a master stone-mason who does amazing work, is booked for months, a bit rude and very expensive. If the look she is known for is worth that price you will be happy. Or perhaps there are two good stone-masons and one is cheaper and available but gets drunk on the job, while another has a wait-list, costs more and is extremely courteous. There are often value-tensions like this and we are happiest when we succeed in the most important areas to us. Be sure and communicate what you know about yourself to your contractor before you sign a contract so that they can factor their bid to give it to you.

Minimizing Construction Impact on Your Lifestyle

This is an important value that is often not considered. While not so common in a landscape project, couples have divorced over home-remodels or new construction when this value is not respected and a stressful construction process is added to an already maxed out marriage or life.

Ways a landscape project can adversely affect your family or lifestyle include:

- Increasing your anxiety about money.

- Arguing over different visions.

- Tension arising when one person makes a last minute change-order without consulting with the other when the design was not well thought out.

- Making parking more difficult when you come home.

- Adding noise, dust, and/or visual chaos to your environment.

- Requiring more of your attention.

If you are doing your landscape project for personal pleasure but it ends up causing you more stress in important areas of your life you will not feel that your project is a success. Things you can do about this include:

- Don't do anything at all. Take half the money you would spend on your landscape and take someone special to a beautiful travel destination!

- Choose a time when you are not already stressed out to do your landscape project.

- Discuss the project thoroughly with your partner and make sure doing something will be a win/win.

- Define construction hours, parking logistics etc. with your contractor up-front (before signing a contract) to make sure that the whole picture of installation is a comfortable one for you.

- Communicate to your contractor what would be ideal for you. For example, for 5-10% more money your contractor may be able to double the size of your crew and have work done in half the time. Or for you it may be the reverse: asking your contractor to work four hour days with a few people and only doing one area at a time could make the project go smoothly and quietly, even if it takes twice as long to finish.

In short, do your job assessing what is most important to you and let those trying to help you know what that is. Most of them won't ask and if you don't volunteer this information the odds go way down of things proceeding in an optimal way for you.

Part Five:

FREE Bonus Material!

Bonus Online Section

I've spent a few hours creating a bonus section for you on my website to add a bit of convenience and visual context. It's not polished or very big. However, if there is something you would particularly like to see, write to me and if it seems like it would be helpful to a number of people I may add to it. You can also always attend one of my classes, where there is at least five minutes for each student to ask questions relating to their specific project.

Go to www.MysticalLandscapes.com/bookbonus to access this free section just for readers of this book.

Community Education Classes

For the past few years I have been teaching landscape classes through the Marin Adult Education program. Information about the current classes can be found at: www.MarinLearn.com. These classes are a terrific way for you to have a personal interaction with me and ask specific questions about your landscape for a very low fee – often around $30.00. This is considerably less than hiring me for a consultation in your garden and gives you a chance to meet other home-owners and learn more about the specific topic.

I've also just started teaching Landscape Design at the College of Marin through their adult education program: www.marin.edu/CommunityEducation.

Classes can be particularly powerful when combined with this book. While there is no substitute for a trained professional giving you their undivided attention in your personal garden, a mixture of this book and a few classes is the next best thing.

In addition to classes I encourage you to visit: www.MarinGardener.org. On this community education site about gardening, sponsored by Mystical Landscapes, you can find all kinds of useful tips and resources in one place.

Hooray! Coupons!

I asked the suppliers I tend to shop at if they would be willing to provide all of you with some coupons to save you some money. Happily for you, some of them said yes and all you need to do is tear off and present the coupons below to save much more money than the book costs!

Note: These must be torn out of the book and presented for one-time use at the time of sale: (More Coupons are available at www.MarinGardener.org)

15% off of one purchase from American Soils (San Rafael Location Only).

$25.00 off your first $100.00 retail at the Urban Farmer.

$15.00 off a $100.00 plant order at Green Jeans Nursery.

Money-Back Guarantee by the Author

If you do not feel it has been worth your time and money to buy and read this book I invite you to receive a full refund. My request is that you help me with my goal of making this book the BEST book for Marin Home-Owners by explaining to me by phone or e-mail the area you found the book did not meet your expectations and any suggestions you have for making it better.

Here's how it works:

- Mail me a copy of the book with your address so I can send you your refund.
- Include any written suggestions you have or include your number so we can talk.
- I may include your suggestions in the next edition.

My address:

Dane E. Rose,
232 Bungalow Ave.
San Rafael, 94901
daneeaster@comcast.net

PS: You don't have to return the book to give feedback. I love to hear both how the book helped you personally and anything you recommend for improvements.

About Mystical Landscapes

It's my goal to counteract the four biggest complaints about the contracting industry in general:

- My work was not done on time.
- It cost more than they said it would.
- They didn't pay attention to what I asked for.
- This did not get talked about until it was too late…

I've been fairly successful at doing just that by doing things differently than most companies:

- I do one job at a time with full attention until complete.
- I accept work in the order it is contracted, which means I sometimes turn down last-minute lucrative jobs that need to be done RIGHT NOW.
- I am both the designer AND foreman on my jobs, insuring that things are installed consistent with my design.
- I use a deadline in my contracts that is realistic and allows for down-time due to weather, crew-shortages or delivery delays.
- I give flat costs for ALL work and stick to those. If something comes up that needs to be done in order to do my bid I include it at no charge so as not to have to ask the client for more money.
- I don't do work for clients who want to skip the design stage (the first mistake or oversight costs everyone more money than the entire design).
- I begin the design process with my detailed landscape questionnaire so that everything that needs to get talked about does get talked about.
- I check in with clients every day or so to make sure that we are all on the same page as the work progresses.

Because 80% of my jobs are done early and ALL of my jobs are done on budget, I recently developed the ONLY three fold landscape guarantee for clients. And because I was surprised at how few people took it seriously (there are so many cost-overruns and delays in construction that some clients are shocked when work is done early and on budget) I've added a pledge to actually PAY YOU money if the work is not done on budget, on time and as specified in our contract. If for any reason I am not able to deliver on this promise I will pay you 10% of the entire installation bid.

There are a list of client responsibilities that relate to this guarantee that I ask clients wanting to formally be a part of this program to agree to. The most important is going through the design process with me and staying with it until I am 100% satisfied that we are all clear and on the same page about what will be done. This is great for me, because I like having happy clients. And while I'm sure it would be nice to avoid some of the concentrated blocks of time needed to develop a good design together, it's good for you too: every mistake avoided will save you hours of stress and money later.

My background in landscaping began in my early teens, working on Organic farms and learning about Biodynamic composting and soil prep. When I started the company at age seventeen I worked alone and for the first two years and did only maintenance. This gives me sensitivity as a designer to doing things in a way that will be easy and practical to maintain.

When client's began asking me to install, I recognized that I learn best with a mentor and went about gathering myself a number of top-of-the-line teachers:

- I worked with one of the leading concrete contractors to learn the basics of pouring and forming up concrete driveways.

- I did extensive consulting with one of the nation's leading septic system designers to learn about how to landscape over septic systems to prolong their life.
- I hired a retired irrigation specialist and landscape architect to train me in the key aspects of irrigation by working with me on my jobs.
- I hired a leading horticulturist who also owned a nursery to answer all my questions about plants on an hourly basis.
- I first hired a great heavy-equipment operator and later practiced on rented heavy equipment until one PG & E engineer complimented me after watching me climb my machine up a steep slope, saying "I don't know any of our operators who could have done that!"
- I became a general contractor and built two custom homes, practicing the technique of saving money by integrating landscaping with the construction project. The first home I built was done on time, only $300.00 over budget, and sold for full-price above appraised value in a sluggish market to a woman who said she bought it because she wanted a home with a nicely integrated landscape and this was the only one on the market.
- I spent some time talking with Architects and two Landscape Architects before developing my own design approach, included in this book.

My training reflects my strengths. I tend to be extremely good at big-picture design and creative problem-solving in very practical and cost-effective ways. I'm terrible at remembering the Latin names of plants. The plants I am really interested in are the few hundred plants that create the most stunning year-round interest. They are all disease-resistant and low maintenance, which saves me the time of having to learn all about plant disease, which is its own specialty.

My best strength is communication. One of my recent clients asked me to be sure and e-mail him about the logistics of the project, commenting that his builder was terrible at that. I did stage one for him and his wife and got it done a day early for a party of his. For the next stage he said: "You know what you are doing so just do it. You are bit TOO GOOD at communicating and I don't have time to read all your e-mails. As long as a client makes their needs known to me, I pay attention to giving them what they want.

This (other than the money of course) is what makes me happy. In that sense I'm more interested in you than in your landscape. I'll be more upset if a client does not get what they were expecting or is not happy than I will be if I think the design could have been better if the client had spent a bit more money. They both matter, but people and feelings are more important than landscapes in my value hierarchy.

And strangely, while this is ideal for many, it is uncomfortable for some who prefer a more detached relationship. I can roll with that, but feel I do my best work for the people I know and understand well.

www.MysticalLandscapes.com